IMITATING
PAUL

LITERARY
CURRENTS
IN
BIBLICAL
INTERPRETATION

EDITORS

Danna Nolan Fewell
Perkins School of Theology,
Southern Methodist University, Dallas TX
David M. Gunn
Columbia Theological Seminary, Decatur GA

EDITORIAL ADVISORY BOARD

Jack Dean Kingsbury
Union Theological Seminary in Virginia, Richmond VA
Peter D. Miscall
St Thomas Seminary, Denver CO
Gary A. Phillips
College of the Holy Cross, Worcester MA
Regina M. Schwartz
Department of English, Duke University, Durham NC
Mary Ann Tolbert
The Divinity School, Vanderbilt University, Nashville TN

IMITATING PAUL

---

a
discourse
of
power

ELIZABETH A. CASTELLI

•

WESTMINSTER/JOHN KNOX PRESS
Louisville, Kentucky

IMITATING PAUL:
A DISCOURSE OF POWER

© 1991 Elizabeth A. Castelli

First edition

Published by Westminster/John Knox Press,
Louisville, Kentucky

PRINTED IN THE UNITED STATES OF AMERICA
2 4 6 8 9 7 5 3 1

Library of Congress Cataloging-in-Publication Data

Castelli, Elizabeth A. (Elizabeth Ann). 1958–
  Imitating Paul : a discourse of power / Elizabeth A. Castelli. — 1st ed.
    p.   cm. — (Literary currents in biblical interpretation)
  Includes bibliographical references and indexes.
  ISBN 0-664-25234-6

  1. Bible.   N.T.   Epistles of Paul—Criticism, interpretation, etc.
2. Mimesis in literature.   3. Power (Social sciences).   I. Title.
II. Series.
BS2650.2.C37 1991
227'.067—dc20   91-30010

To the Memory of my Father, Lou Castelli
and to my Mother, Rosemarie Castelli
who both have long endured my insistence
on the value of difference

CONTENTS

SERIES
PREFACE

New currents in biblical interpretation are emerging. Questions about origins—authors, intentions, settings—and stages of composition are giving way to questions about the literary qualities of the Bible, the play of its language, the coherence of its final form, and the relations between text and readers.

Such literary criticism is rapidly acquiring sophistication as it learns from major developments in secular critical theory, especially in understanding the instability of language and the key role of readers in the production of meaning. Biblical critics are being called to recognize that a plurality of readings is an inevitable and legitimate consequence of the interpretive process. By the same token, interpreters are being challenged to take responsibility for the theological, social, and ethical implications of their readings.

Biblical interpretation is changing on the practical as well as the theoretical level. More readers, both inside and outside the academic guild, are discovering that the Bible in literary perspective can powerfully engage people's lives. Communities of faith where the Bible is foundational may find that literary criticism can make the Scripture accessible in a way that historical criticism seems unable to do.

Within these changes lie exciting opportunities for all who seek contemporary meaning in the ancient texts. The goal of the series is to encourage such change and such search, to breach the confines of traditional biblical criticism, and to open channels for new currents of interpretation.

—THE EDITORS

ACKNOWLEDGMENTS

This book, in somewhat different contour, had a previous incarnation as a dissertation at Claremont Graduate School a number of years ago. At that point, my advisor Burton L. Mack was the gracious and patient mentor who performed that delicate balancing act of encouraging and challenging the project, pushing me to test the limits of my discourse and urging me to think broadly while still attending to crucial details. More than anyone, he has helped me make sense of my place in the discourse about religion; and his gifts of support, humor, perspective, and friendship are still treasured possessions I carry with me. My other teachers, the late Horst R. Moehring of Brown University, Bernadette J. Brooten (now of Harvard University), James M. Robinson, and Vincent L. Wimbush (now at Union Theological Seminary), have, I hope, left traces of their contributions to my education on this text.

Other colleagues have been sources of commentary, critique, and support in the reworking of this project. I especially wish to thank Hal Taussig for his patient (re)readings (especially of the last chapter), his scandalous optimism and good humor, and his enthusiastic assurances that in some way this text answers some of the "so what?" questions intellectual work most often leaves hanging; Gary Phillips, for his careful reading and very helpful commentary on the original manuscript; Tikva Frymer-Kensky, for her reading of and helpful suggestions for the last chapter; and the working group of which I have now been a part for some time, consisting of George Aichele, Fred Burnett, Bob Fowler, David Jobling, Stephen Moore, Tina Pippin, and Wilhelm Wuellner. While this group has not had a direct relationship to this particular text, it has been a constant reminder of the collegial context in which new ways of reading the biblical text can be interrogated, explored, and experimented with; the work of these different people makes this particular project feel less isolated. Finally, I would also like to thank Danna Nolan

Fewell and David M. Gunn, the co-editors of this series, for their support and gracious advocacy of the volume.

The theoretical orientation of this volume harkens back to an earlier period of my life, when we were all reading Foucault and Derrida just to keep up with conversation over the dinner table: those conversations (and meals) were graced by the wits and intelligence of Bill Wharton, Byron Hammer, Elizabeth Weed, Christina Crosby, and Mary Renda, and I'm delighted that most of those conversations are still going on. Later, Lee Klosinski became a pleasing participant in the conversation as well as a constant dinner companion; he continues to offer the gifts of his intellect, his friendship, and his spirited humor.

My biggest debt in my professional life in general, and in the production of this book in particular, is to the unyielding moral and material support of my family: my sister, Teresa, and my parents, Lou and Rosemarie Castelli. It is ironic to note, in a book that deals with issues of power and identity, the overarching debt I owe to these people in relationship to whom my own claims to power and identity cannot help but be framed. My parents in particular have experienced over the years the reverberations of my emerging commitments to critiques of power, interrogations of the tyrannies of economies of sameness, and the embracing of differences. As we have struggled through together with equal displays of exasperation, generosity, humor, and love, I am more convinced each day that my positions have developed, not in opposition to those of my family, but are rooted in the best lessons taught to me by my family—especially those about taking pleasure in both the work and the struggle, about trying to maintain some sense of clarity concerning what is really important, and most crucially about remembering occasionally at least not to take oneself completely seriously. It is one of the great regrets of my life that my father did not live to see this book in print, and I only hope that, whatever shortcomings the text holds, they are small enough that Lou's recurrent and multi-purpose admonition to me—"Don't sweat the little things, kid!"—will hold firm. I dedicate this book to his irrepressible memory, and to the ongoing strength of my mother.

—ELIZABETH A. CASTELLI

INTRODUCTION

Pious imitation of others has long been central to the history of Christian practice. Exhortations to struggle to attain the perfection of the saints, for example, have resonated in the religious formation of generations of Catholic children, second only to exhortations to translate suffering and disappointment into spiritual currency by "offering it up." This study was sparked, somewhat playfully at first, by what struck me as a remarkable paradox in relation to this central dimension of Christian piety and ideology. On the one hand, imitation has always seemed self-evidently inscribed in a hierarchical relationship of power: one imitates saints, for example, because they are of course better, closer to God, and more holy (usually because they had the good fortune to be born in more heroic and dramatic times, and consequently had more occasions to face down beasts in the arena or to demonstrate in other near-miraculous ways their devotion). It goes virtually without saying that the very practice of imitation dooms one to failure. One may want to be like the saints, to take on that identity of holiness, but ultimately, those gestures are at best shadowy approximations of the fuller, more complete, indeed perfect gestures of one's models. (Cynicism is not the preferred response to one's inevitable failure, of course; failure becomes the reason to strive still more fervently!)

The paradox lies in juxtaposing this self-evident observation to the modern interpretations of the earliest Christian exhortations to imitation, found in Paul's letters. To read these interpretations, imitating Paul has nothing to do with power relations, and everything to do with social expediency or the benign observation that Paul was obviously a special figure to the early churches, so why should one not attempt to align oneself with his position?

Even given the (considerable temporal and formal) distance between the colorful images of later saints and the blander and more severe image of Paul which emerges from his letters—as models go, Paul possesses precious little pizzazz—and even given Paul's remarkable uniqueness as the only self-proclaimed model in the tradition, the almost total silence of modern scholarship on the relationship of imitation to power seemed quite strange to me. As I began to read and think further about these questions, I became more and more engaged with the philosophical questions concerning the problems of imitation and identity, and the ways in which they relate to questions of power. Mimesis (imitation), the relationship between the model and its copy, has been the object of critical analysis in Western thought from the pre-Socratics to the post-structuralists, raising fundamental questions about representation and identity.[1] In focusing on a particular moment in the history of mimesis, I have taken on a more modest task than that of philosophical speculation. Rather, I wish to interpret a particular series of articulations of mimesis in order to ask questions about their ideological effects.

Mimesis appears in the earliest Christian writings in Paul's exhortations to the Christians to whom he writes to become his imitators, to enter into a mimetic relationship with him as the model. These exhortations have been variously interpreted by scholars, who have generally tried to show that Paul's use of the notion of imitation ties him to the dominant rhetorical and ethical traditions of his day or to the theological traditions of the imitation of Christ (*imitatio Christi*). While much of this research has provided a useful background study of mimesis, in the "history of ideas" tradition, it has done little to illuminate the question of the systemic function of mimesis. Nor has it asked how such exhortations might have affected the social formation of the nascent Christian communities to which Paul wrote. Indeed there is a paradoxical, inverse relationship between the preponderance of references to, articulations of, and claims to power in early Christian texts, and the relative silence of interpreters in taking up questions of the power relations underwritten or enabled by these texts. This book is a gesture towards engaging that paradox, an attempt to examine what

Foucault might well call New Testament scholarship's great "unthought."

The thesis of this study is that the notion of mimesis functions in Paul's letters as a strategy of power. That is, it articulates and rationalizes as true and natural a particular set of power relations within the social formation of early Christian communities.

In what follows, the first chapter will take seriously the ideological dimensions of Paul's writings. It will discuss how much biblical interpretation often elides claims to truth with truth itself, how significant discussion of the problematics of power is remarkably absent from the study of New Testament texts, and finally, how problematic are the studies of imitation in Paul that do not admit to ideological interests either of the author or of the reader.

From this critique of the present state of inquiry, chapter two offers an alternative theoretical position, basic to the rest of the study. This position examines the relationship, which is an interactive one, between discourse (the source texts) and social formations (the early Christian movements), using Paul's appropriation of mimesis as an example. This chapter will provide a brief introduction to the work of Michel Foucault, whose analyses of "regimes of truth" and "technologies of power" provide the interpretive lens for the present study. While not putting forward a comprehensive sociological model against which to test "early Christianity," this chapter will make explicit certain theoretical presuppositions that govern the following interpretive chapters. These include presuppositions about power relations in social networks; about the relationship between texts, discourse, and rhetoric, on the one hand, and social formations on the other; and about the ways in which reading discourse with its social effects in mind makes a difference for reconstructing early Christian social experience as well as its continuing effects.

Chapter three sketches a brief history of the notion of mimesis in antiquity. The goal here is not to produce a univocal definition of mimesis, but rather to describe a range and field of significance for the term. Mimesis permeates ancient discourses, and this chapter will briefly address its function within the religious realm (in dramatic ritual reenactment and in the attempts to assimilate to the divine), the cosmological realm (in which the universe is understood to be a lesser reflection and imitation of the divine order), the realm of political theory (where the king-philosopher is cast as the privileged imitator of the divine), the aesthetic realm (where nature and culture are related mimetically, and classical authors are related to their successors in a struggle for an authoritative voice), and the worlds of rhetoric, education, and ethics (where the most successful students are the best imitators of their teachers).

Out of this survey of the ancient discourses of mimesis will come a series of generalizations about the notion of imitation which Paul inherited from Greco-Roman culture:

(1) Mimesis is always articulated as a hierarchical relationship, whereby the "copy" is but a derivation of the "model" and cannot aspire to the privileged status of the "model."

(2) Mimesis presupposes a valorization of sameness over against difference. Certain conceptual equations accompany this move: unity and harmony are associated with sameness while difference is attributed characteristics of diffusion, disorder, and discord.

(3) The notion of the authority of the model plays a fundamental role in the mimetic relationship.

The goal of chapter four is to produce close readings of the texts in Paul's letters which invoke the notion of imitation (1 Thess 1:6, 2:14; Phil 3:17; 1 Cor 4:16, 11:1). These readings will attempt to show how imitation reinforces certain ideas about social relations within the Christian community and the relationship of those ideas to Christian truth. My argument is that Paul has appropriated a notion of mimesis completely naturalized within first-century culture, so that the term mimesis would evoke for his original audiences the rich set of associations sketched out in the previous chapter. Paul's use of the rhetoric of mimesis is not simply the benign call to emulate a laudable ethical model, as some have argued, nor does it represent some self-evident social pragmatism, as others have asserted. Rather, Paul's command, "Be imitators of me," evokes a complex structural and thematic weave that resists reduction to any sort of self-evident or obvious ethical action or social expediency. At the root of this exhortation is a far more profoundly embedded understanding of the privileged position of the apostle to construct the early communities within a hierarchical "economy of sameness," the structuring of thought and social life around the uniquely valued concept of *identity*. Furthermore, the exhortation to imitation underwrites the apostle's demand for the erasure of difference, and links that erasure to the very possibility of salvation. It will be argued that, in this way, mimesis functions, in Paul's writings, as a discourse of power, as the reinscription of power relations within the social formation of early Christian communities.

Chapter five will raise the question of what difference a reading self-conscious in the analysis of power and ideology makes, especially for the dynamics of imitation the book explores. In examining the reading effects of Paul's discourse, a discourse that occupies an important place in the master narratives of Western culture, I want to ask how Paul's "economy of sameness" resonates in Western culture. That is to say, this chapter will explore the underside of Pauline discourse (and, by extension, the Christian master narrative of which that discourse is a central part), namely its apparent inability to sustain difference, and ask the question—what is at stake in that inability, what is lost?

It is hoped that this book will contribute to New Testament scholarship in two important ways. First of all, it opens up for examination and discussion what I have come to call the "fallacy of self-evidence." By this term I mean a rhetorical move and the more general hermeneutical position undergirding that move, both of which have to do with unexamined and implicit assumptions about the way early Christian social relations must have been constructed. For one thing, scholarship has a remarkable propensity for reconstructing early Christian history as a kind of mirror image of its own social setting, or in accordance with its own tastes about what the origins of the church should look like. The most poignant example of this is the marvelous collection of biographies of Jesus which emerged from the original quest for the historical Jesus, but such mirroring is equally common in other scholarly reconstructions of early Christian communities. In a similar vein, there appears to be a persistent psychologizing aspect to some reconstructions, in which some rhetorical move on Paul's part, for example, is explained in terms of a kind of "natural response to a difficult situation," implying both a unified human nature and a singular mode of social experience. That such a move should have been undertaken goes without saying; furthermore the regimes of truth and relations of power that enable and sustain them are not questioned. Both of these aspects of the fallacy of self-evidence are as prevalent in scholarship as they are due suspicion in a critical inquiry. This volume seeks to avoid the problems of either reading back into early Christian experience or psychologizing, by refocusing the inquiry around questions of *discursive constructions* of social relations.

The second contribution I hope this study makes to scholarship is the interpretation itself, the product of experimenting with another way of reading the text. The process of close reading is in itself not a particularly new one for biblical criticism, but perhaps the way in which it will be performed here is different. The process will focus on textual effect rather than on any (fictional) inherent meaning in the text, or in other words, on how the text operates rather than what it means. The results of this way of reading will cast the theme of imitation in Paul in quite a different light. That recasting may well suggest a way in which the rhetoric of social experience in early Christian discourses and practices might be seen differently and, perhaps, more clearly. It is to that general end that I dedicate my study.

IMITATING
PAUL

1

IMITATION AND PROBLEMS OF POWER, IDEOLOGY, AND INTERPRETATION

IMITATION, POWER, AND IDENTITY

What does it mean to imitate? In what fields of meaning is "imitation" inscribed? What are its ideological resonances? What meanings does it repress? The notion of imitation presupposes at least two important and related things: a relationship between at least two elements and, within that relationship, the progressive movement of one of those elements to become similar to or the same as the other. This relationship is asymmetrical, for imitation does not involve both elements moving simultaneously toward similarity, but rather one element being fixed and the other transforming itself or being transformed into an approximation of the first. The favored movement is from difference toward similarity—or, ideally and absolutely, toward sameness. Sameness itself becomes a more highly valued quality, and it is a quality which automatically inheres in the model in the mimetic relationship of model–copy. Because in the texts under consideration a mimetic relationship is not simply being described but is actually being exhorted into being, the sameness that is valued here takes on a normative character. In other words, sameness is not merely described, but rather it is pre-scribed.

The ideological force of such a prescription is clear; if imitation and the drive toward sameness are exhorted and celebrated, then difference is perceived as problematic, danger-ous, threatening. Further, the prescription of sameness implies the repression of difference. Why? The practice of imitation is a theoretical focus on sameness concurrent with a literal focusing on it. As the copy continues to remake itself or to be remade in ever more closely approximating images of the model, the same-ness of the model is continually reinscribed. At the same time, the sameness of the model is continually imbued with more and more importance because it becomes the center of activity, the norm against which deviance is measured. The paradox of imitation, articulated first in Plato's indictment of the imitative arts, that imitation can never absolutely succeed, only under-writes further the asymmetry of the mimetic struggle and its fixation on the privileged and normative status of the model.

Imitation is then a celebration of identity, in the sense that sameness implies the quality of identicalness. It is the struggle to write the identity of the model onto the copy. Further, imitation implies, then, a critical relationship of power, insofar as the model represents the standard toward which its copies move. The model sets the terms of the relationship, which is both hierarchical and asymmetrical.

The ideology of imitation is articulated within the fields of both social relations (power) and metaphysics (identity). Given the importance of the notion in the Pauline corpus in the New Testament, one might easily be drawn to think that such fields would be explicitly interrogated in the study of these texts; remarkably, they are rarely critically engaged. Instead, the ideology of imitation is apparently so naturalized and the power relations articulated more generally in the New Testament are so taken for granted by its interpreters, that questions of power and identity are only occasionally broached.

SKIRTING THE QUESTION OF POWER

The verb "to skirt" has several meanings, and obviously the formulation of the title above implies two of these which are related: "to go around or keep away from in order to avoid danger or discovery" and "to avoid because of difficulty or fear of controversy." A third meaning resonates here, "to be, lie, or move along an edge, border, or margin" (Webster 1988:1105). For just as many commentators on the New Testament have skirted the question of power—to avoid danger or for fear of controversy—so the question of power has continued to skirt both the text and commentaries upon it, bordering them, filling up the margins, framing the texts. Though early Christian texts are full of references to, articulations of, and claims to power, paradoxically the interpretation of these texts rarely has taken up the question of the power relations underwritten or enabled by these texts, or examined the implications of power being enacted discursively. When power is discussed, the relations it inscribes are largely taken for granted. Until quite recently, the ideological character of the texts under consideration has rarely been examined and even more rarely acknowledged. This study takes seriously the ideological assumptions and gestures present in Paul's writings, and attempts to examine some of their effects. This chapter will articulate the reasons for such an analysis, in part by examining briefly the interpretations already available of the texts under discussion.

   In Pauline scholarship on mimesis, at least two moves have been operative, both of which either remarkably skirt the question of power or reinscribe it unproblematically. The first move involves a spiritualizing gesture towards the text, one which, not incidentally, assumes the transparency of textual reference while remaining silent on the question of the interestedness of the text. The second move stems from an implicit investment in the notion of the tradition itself as authoritative, monolithic, and univocal. Where there may be evidence for competing interpretations of power in the text, this interpretive gesture authorizes one and mutes the others. In this move, the texts seem to be taken as a univocal signifier of authority, rather than as a site at which power is negotiated, brokered, or inscribed—or even as a record of that conflict. This interpretive gesture authorizes the text's claims to power, thereby performing an analogous move to that figured in the mimetic relationship itself: just as the copy's focus on the model continuously reinscribes the model's authority, so commentary on the discourse of imitation which is oblivious to the problems of power reinscribes the text's own self-authorization. The commentator's text itself enters into a mimetic relationship with the model text, and *power*, as a textual effect, is merged with the text's own *assertions about power.*

The discussion which follows does not offer an exhaustive review of the scholarly literature dedicated to Paul's use of the idea of imitation. Such a review might well be obfuscating for the general reader while superfluous for the expert.[1] What is more relevant for this discussion is an analysis of some of the representative studies within this broader group, analysis which highlights the two interpretive moves described above: first, the spiritualizing gesture that skirts the question of power; and second, the mimetic gesture, which reinscribes the textual effects of power and thereby authorizes the text's claims to truth as truth. What will become clear is that these moves are not always separable, but reinforce each other at points even while they are not completely coterminous. The rest of this chapter, then, will look at these two interpretive moves, and then rearticulate the question of the ideological effects of Paul's discourse of imitation, pointing ahead to the Foucauldian framing of this present study in chapter two.

Spiritualizing Imitation/Skirting Power

One of the interpretive strategies encountered frequently in readings of imitation in Paul's letters is an attempt to uncover a pattern of continuity between Paul's discourses and those of both earlier texts and later traditions. Two tactics are striking: the alignment of Paul's exhortations to imitation with historically prior (if narrated later) traditions of "following Jesus" and earlier Hebrew Bible themes (usually read through Greek lenses), and the move to situate Paul's exhortations at the root of the later spirituality or piety of *imitatio Christi*.[2] What seems to be at stake here is a desire to demonstrate an absolute kind of continuity of tradition, not only between the gospels and Paul, but also between the Hebrew Bible and the New Testament. The smoothness of the movement from one set of texts and cultural contexts to another ought to strike even the marginally critical reader as at least somewhat odd.

Tinsley's work on the contribution to Christian spirituality of the notion of *imitatio Christi* is a classic case in point for this form of interpretation which spiritualizes the notion of imitation (making it abstract and situating it as a spiritual exercise rather than as also a social relation). His work is not concerned particularly with textual interpretation or historical reconstruction, but rather attempts to construct a sweeping continuity with earlier material. Tinsley is interested in demonstrating an authentic biblical mysticism, in which the historical act and actor, and the reality to which they refer, are collapsed into a single sign (Tinsley 1960:21). With respect to the relevant biblical texts, Tinsley argues that Jesus becomes an imitator of Israel whose following in the ways of God is documented in the Hebrew Bible; Jesus' disciples imitate him, and the pattern is repeated by Paul, who imitates Christ and who calls the early communities to imitate him.[3] Tinsley's discourse about the texts on imitation shows that he sees the text as an absolutely transparent reference to the "reality" it narrates; there is no distance between the text and the "reality" to which it refers. The continuity self-consciously narrated by the evangelists between the Hebrew Bible and the life of Jesus is read by Tinsley not as a discursive strategy to situate early Christian practices within the discursive range of the earlier traditions, but rather as a relationship that is simply self-evident and true. The text functions as a mere record of the relentless and singular march of salvation history, which starts with God and ends with Christian salvation. Imitation plays a constitutive role in creating this singular and comprehensive experience; it is at the heart of the mysticism Tinsley seeks to identify.

All of the works on *imitatio Christi* assume a fundamental level of continuity between the idea of following Jesus and imitating Christ. This insistence on viewing these notions as continuous with each other—and, in some cases, continuous with a proposed idea of *imitatio dei* in the Hebrew Bible—is rooted in a theological desire to view history itself as a singular, unilateral voyage toward Christian salvation. Here, the commitment to the notion of continuity joins together with the view of the text as referential to produce a vision of imitation skirting (or eliding) the question of power.[4] Power becomes unthought or unthinkable in this reading of imitation, because a series of questions about the relationship between the text and the social forces that made its production possible have been bracketed or rendered unaskable. This process of bracketing makes sense only if one understands the text to be the result of some divine intervention into social life, that is, as unexplainable at the level of social theory. These interpretations see the text as a free-floating empty vessel bearing a set of ideas that have some undefined claim to universalism. Because these positions underplay, and in some cases deny, the historical specificity of any text's production and interpretation, they correlatively minimize or rule out consideration of the possibility that there is any relevant interaction between social forces and discourse. It is in this way that they render power unthinkable.

Authorizing and Unifying Tradition as the Reinscription of Power

An alternative or a supplement to rendering power unthinkable in analyses of Paul's discourses of imitation has been to render it natural, self-evident, something which goes virtually without saying. It is this practice that is undertaken by the majority of interpreters of these passages. Specifically, the argument—or often, the assumption—is that the relations Paul underwrites in his discourse of imitation contribute to the simple, straightforward construction of a univocal tradition. This kind of explanation can be found in the earliest scholarly discussion of mimesis in the Pauline corpus, where imitation and a piety of obedience to the models of Christ, God, and, by association, Paul are linked in the focusing of a singular tradition. For Michaelis, for example, imitation "is not repetition of a model. It is an expression of obedience" (Michaelis 1967:668).[5] What is striking about this argument is that Michaelis does not appear to connect his reading of the call to obedience he ascribes to Paul's discourse of mimesis to the broader context of Paul's larger rhetorical agenda. That is, he does not make any suggestions concerning the implications of mimesis for authority in general in the early communities to which Paul writes. In avoiding both a rhetorical and a social reading he reinscribes the power relations implied and argued for in the text as though they were already in place and unquestioned.

This same kind of interpretive gesture appears in the later work of Willis Peter de Boer who, in treating the question of the imitation of Paul, reads Paul's call for imitation as a natural and obvious expression of Paul's concern for his spiritual children in the communities which he founded.[6] De Boer describes the content of imitation as "humility, self-denial, self-giving, self-sacrifice for the sake of Christ and the salvation of others" (de Boer 1962:207). He goes on to suggest that the emphasis on the specificity of the imitation of *Paul*, as opposed to imitation of Christ, is grounded in the fact that Paul is attempting to protect true Christianity from heretical incursions within the communities to which he writes. De Boer articulates his position in this way:

> Paul's call to imitation is not in order to secure certain Pauline characteristics in the Christianity that is coming to expression in his readers. The characteristics which must come to expression are those basic to Christianity itself. Paul is not making special pleas for his version of Christianity and his manner of Christian life. We can not agree with Stanley's proposal that Paul's call for the imitation of himself arises from there being something unique about his Christianity. (de Boer 1962:209)

A basic theoretical presupposition here is that there was such a thing as "Christianity" which could at this moment in history be termed "true" or "false," a pre-existing, singular, authorized tradition that therefore authorized Paul's apparent attempts to underwrite his particular view of how things ought to be done in Christian communities. De Boer's notion of "Christianity itself" seems to suggest that what eventually surfaces as "the tradition"—and it remains arguable whether that is ever all that is travelling under the banner of the proper name, even after a certain hegemony has been established—somehow already is in existence at the very early moments at which Paul is writing. Rather than asserting or presuming the existence of such an authorizing tradition, I am arguing for reading early Christian discourses and practices *historically*, in all their multiplicity and diffusion. Further, I am suggesting that, even in a text that eventually becomes part of the hegemonic dominant discourse (i.e., the canon, and a particularly privileged part of it at that), there remain resonances of competing discourses whose dismissal out of hand begs the question of power. That is to say, while one might well read and interpret Paul's discourse as one voice in the debate, to assign his discourse the value of reflecting characteristics which are "basic to Christianity itself" is to deny the rhetoricity, the perspectival nature, of his discourse. Further, the invocation of language about heresy[7] concerning these early communities is an anachronistic theological gesture which has lost its justification with Bauer's classic challenge to the categories of "orthodoxy" and "heresy" (Bauer 1934).

A rather different study of these questions of the relationship of imitation to the tradition may be found in Hans Dieter Betz's 1967 study, *Nachfolge und Nachahmung Jesu Christi im Neuen Testament*, in many ways a more theologically oriented study of the notions of following and imitation in the New Testament. Adopting the observations of Schulz (1962), who distinguishes between the notion of "following" (*akolouthein*) in the gospel traditions and "imitation" in the Pauline corpus, Betz seeks to explore the question of theological continuity and discontinuity embodied in the "following"-"imitation" distinction. The thesis he articulates is that, despite the clear philological discontinuity between the notion of discipleship (following Jesus) in the gospels and the notion of mimesis (imitation of Paul [Christ]) in Paul, one must not necessarily discard the possibility of continuity at the level of intention. That is, discipleship in both contexts has the same theological significance, obedience to God's will (Betz 1967:3).

Betz shares Schulz's conclusions that the *akolouthein* language of the gospels stems from a Palestinian-Jewish origin, while arguing that the "history and structure" of the notion of mimesis are clearly Hellenistic (Betz 1967:3). Furthermore, his insights into the cultic origins of mimesis language—and the implications for later use of the language of mimesis, that is, that mimesis is to be understood as representation of reality and not reality itself—are illuminating.

Betz ultimately comes to a theological conclusion—that a singular type of discipleship (obedience to God) is the ultimate, continuous, and univocal referent of both the *akolouthein* language of the gospels and the *mimêsis* language of the Pauline corpus. In reaching this conclusion, Betz joins with the others who have engaged in the continuity-discontinuity discussions in ultimately underwriting a singular vision of the tradition. At the same time, he presupposes that it is possible to collapse the philological differences between *akolouthein* and *mimêsis* in favor of a monolithic "intention." Such a move produces several effects. First, it appears to harmonize and homogenize early Christian discourse. The specificity of Pauline discourse of mimesis is veiled by the more overarching hermeneutical conclusion that, whatever polyvalent language is used, a univocal notion of discipleship is the clear referent of all of it. Second, such a move helps to undergird the claims to authority that the text makes by reasserting them. It participates, in other words, in a mimetic relationship with Paul's text analogous to the mimetic relationship into which Paul exhorts the early communities to enter.

The biggest difficulty in all of these readings is that they create no ironic distance between the readings of the text and the text itself. This limitation in the scholarly discourse on mimesis will only be repeated in virtually all of the studies of imitation which situate imitation more specifically within apostolic tradition[8] or which see imitation as primarily an ethical expectation,[9] since they are essentially derivative of and dependent upon these earlier and more specialized works on imitation.

Two exceptions to this generalized characterization should, at the same time, be highlighted. One sophisticated attempt to deal with the question of the construction of authority in Pauline rhetoric may be found in the work of John Howard Schütz. In this work, Schütz attempts to discuss the larger questions of the nature of the authority upon which Paul's discourse depends, and to look at the ways in which Paul's authority is grounded in his own understanding of his own normativeness. What is of particular interest here to the current inquiry is the way in which Schütz understands the function of imitation as part of "The Rhetoric of Apostolic Authority" (Schütz 1975:204-248).

The image by which Schütz renders the sense of mimesis in Paul's writing is that of *reflection*. This is in contrast to Michaelis's reading of mimesis as a demand for obedience, but it also accords the mimetic relationship a level of complexity. First, it takes seriously the nature of mimesis as the creation of some kind of analogy between the model and the copy. Second, it accounts for the authoritative aspect of mimesis: the role of the privileged authority of Paul.[10]

Benjamin Fiore, in his dissertation on the uses of example in the Socratic and Pastoral epistles, takes up the question of apostolic tradition, exploring it through the lens of Greek and Roman rhetorical categories. He includes a chapter on Paul's use of personal example, which takes as its point of departure Michaelis's *TDNT* article (discussed above). He then interprets Paul's exhortations of imitation in terms of the rhetorical patterns he has outlined in earlier chapters. He concludes that Paul is very much grounded in the rhetorical traditions of the surrounding culture, and that Paul's calls to imitation should be read through this pattern of example.[11]

Fiore's erudition and careful reading of the rhetorical tradition are both striking, and the connections he makes between the rhetorical tradition and Paul's use of hortatory devices are well-justified and convincingly argued. The difficulty presented by Fiore's argument vis-à-vis Paul's discourse of mimesis is that it seems to cast certain distinctions in terms which are too harsh and its point is overdrawn. Fiore's basic argument is cast against Michaelis's conclusions—that the call to imitation is basically a call to obedience. In attempting to undercut Michaelis's argument, Fiore neglects a fundamental aspect of the discourse of mimesis in antiquity, that is, the authority with which the model is implicitly imbued, as I demonstrate in chapter 3. This is not to argue that the discourse of mimesis does not also possess an emulative (imitative) aspect as well, and Fiore has outlined this aspect carefully. It is remarkable however that Fiore, whose argument is so dependent on notions drawn from rhetoric, would dismiss the authoritative aspect of the mimetic relationship, which is the very aspect that gives the discourse of mimesis its rhetorical thrust.[12]

What ties these studies together is their interest in the relationship between the notion of imitation and the idea of apostolic tradition and authority. Here, the rhetoric of the discourse of imitation is highlighted by some, Schütz and Fiore, especially, though neither of these presses the question of rhetorical *effect* of the discourse. Their major contribution to the investigation of the nature of mimesis in early Christian discourse and practice is that they begin, albeit timidly, to position the question in terms of social formation.

The work that connects imitation to ethical issues manages more often than not to reduce the complexity of imitation, highlighted in the more thorough works, to a few simple assertions about what is at stake in the mimetic relationship. One example will suffice: Victor Paul Furnish, an important researcher into the nature of Pauline ethics, dedicates a half-dozen pages to the consideration of the question of mimesis. His conclusions are tantalizingly stated and abandoned; he does not follow through to consider the implications of his statements concerning mimesis. First, he observes that

> it is clear that Paul regards himself not only as a bearer of
> *traditions* but also as a bearer of Christ. . . . To imitate Paul
> and Christ means to conform to Christ's suffering and death in
> the giving of one's self over to the service of others. (Furnish
> 1968:222-223)

While this does draw Furnish to conclude that Paul's ethic is radically christocentric (Furnish 1968:224), it says nothing about the privileged position that Paul has implicitly claimed for himself. It reinscribes a confusion of identity between Paul and Christ ("to imitate Paul and Christ means to conform to Christ's suffering and death . . . ") which is, in fact, extremely important for the whole mimetic economy in the Pauline epistles, but it does so without inserting any ironic distance between Paul's writing about his confusion of identity and the reader's reading about it.

Furnish's second conclusion about the nature of imitation in Pauline discourse is that

> it is noteworthy that none of these imitation passages singles out any particular qualities of the earthly Jesus with the insistence that they be emulated. Rather, it seems always to be the humble, giving, obedient *love* of the crucified and resurrected Lord to which the final appeal is made. (Furnish 1968: 223)

This conclusion is remarkably suggestive, not at the level of theological ethics where Furnish has positioned it, but at the level of the rhetorical impact of the call to imitation. That is, the call to imitation has no particular content. Furnish reads that contentless quality of the object of imitation to express a persistent (though unarticulated) reference to the crucifixion. Another way of considering this lack of content, though, might be more fruitful at the level of constructions of social power and of the rhetorical effect of the text. Furnish is right that the object of imitation is remarkably imprecise, but his explanation for the imprecision is unconvincing. I will argue, in contrast, that the lack of content of the object of imitation is itself a rhetorical gesture which both reinforces the power of Paul's example and implicates the imitators in the economy of sameness by forcing them always to be "policing" themselves, because their model is conspicuously imprecise.

TRADITION AS IDEOLOGY

The critique levelled here against a number of the studies addressing the question of imitation is that they have either spiritualized imitation or naturalized it, and that in so doing, they either have ignored the implicit articulation of power present in the advocacy of mimetic relations or have rendered the power relationship unproblematic and self-evident. There is a continuing interest in the interpretive discourses surrounding the imitation texts in Paul in demonstrating and reinscribing a singularity within "the tradition." These gestures of demonstration and reinscription place the interpretations in a mimetic relation to the Pauline text, analogous to the mimetic relationship Paul himself seeks to institute with the communities to which he writes. The results are several: Paul's discourse, which is situational, rhetorical, embattled to lesser and greater degrees, and in competition with other discourses, is imbued by later interpreters with the hegemonic status it seeks to claim. Therefore, the relations his discourse seeks to inscribe in the social lives of early Christian communities are likewise underwritten by that discursive authority. Meanwhile, tradition is viewed as something monolithic, univocal, and almost preordained, rather than as an ideological construct or a contested terrain. The result is, as I have noted before, either a blurring of power relations or a reinscription of them. In either case, they remain naturalized and uninterrogated.

In contrast to the dominant interpretive discourse, it is one of the grounding assumptions of this study that tradition is not the simple articulation of monolithic truth, but is itself the product of discourse and ideology. This is not to minimize the power of tradition in shaping consciousness, nor to articulate a counterclaim that is superior because of its opposition. Rather it is to point out that the very notion of a totalizing, fully explanatory system of meaning (tradition) is itself ideological, not self-evident. Given this silence of the interpretive voices on the questions of ideology and power, it strikes me that some alternative approach to the problem of power in the mimetic relationship as it is advocated in Pauline discourse is required.

2

THEORETICAL
FRAMEWORKS:
FOUCAULT
AND
POWER

As we have seen, the notion of power in early Christian discourse has been given remarkably little attention. In particular, New Testament studies have ignored the social effect of the rhetoric of power. This failure stems both from a refusal to investigate the ideological effects of (biblical or interpretive) discourse and from certain theological presuppositions about the nature of Pauline discourse and its relationship to other early Christian discourses and to the Hebrew Bible.

My study attempts to move in a different direction. Here early Christian practices and discourses are not assumed to be structurally unique over against any other social formation at any other moment in history. This is not to collapse differences or to downplay the particularities of early Christian social formation. Rather, it is to challenge the "specialness" usually attributed to early Christianity—an attribution which masks a theological claim to a privileged truth for Christianity and a concern to uncover, at the "origins" of Christianity, a particularly pristine version of that truth. My focus on Paul is a matter of necessity, because his texts are the earliest coherent expression of what one might call an early Christian position. In contrast to some other interpreters, I do not attempt to privilege

Paul's viewpoint or position. I do, however, claim that Paul himself does just that and that later tradition reinscribes this privilege. I focus on his discourse specifically because he *claims* the position of the privileged speaker for these nascent Christian communities, and such a claim in and of itself has profound social implications—whether these are rationalized through theological justifications or by any other means.

I do not intend to present a full-blown and comprehensive model of social formation. Rather, I wish to redescribe and reinterpret a particular example of early Christian discourse which advocates an ideal set of social relations. This attempt at redescription and reinterpretation is based upon a series of presuppositions about the relationship between discourse and social exchange, about the rhetorical nature of any text (particularly one as "authoritative" as Paul's), and about the social/political effects of rhetoric.

FOUCAULT AND POWER

The political and social processes by which the Western European societies were put in order are not very apparent, have been forgotten, or have become habitual. They are a part of our most familiar landscape, and we don't perceive them anymore. But most of them once scandalized people. It is one of my targets to show people that a lot of things that are a part of their landscape—that people think are universal—are the result of some very precise historical changes. All my analyses are against the idea of universal necessities in human existence. They show the arbitrariness of institutions and show which space of freedom we can still enjoy and how many changes can still be made. (Foucault in R. Martin 1988:11)

When Michel Foucault spoke these words, he was just beginning to tap the rich sources of the Western cultural inheritance embodied in early Christian literature. But if his words are meaningful for the period stretching from the classical age of the eighteenth century to the present, they are also resonant and suggestive for earlier periods, when Western ideas about truth, language, and transcendence were being fixed and rendered obvious and imperceptible.

I agree with Foucault that the production of cultural assumptions is a historical process that can be rendered visible
through interpretation. With Foucault, I reject the notion that
there is anything universally human about cultural and social
formations and institutions. Societies are organized and power
relations emerge in response to very particular historical circumstances. Social formations and institutions are not inevitable
forms produced by human necessity, but rather are changeable
and arbitrary—though they may well adhere to a particular
logic found to be more or less persuasive at particular moments.
Nevertheless, human being itself is not a singular, monolithic
category. The concept of the "human" (articulated in modern
philosophy as "man") is itself a cultural production and by no
means self-evident. Part of my project here is aimed at revealing
the humanist assumptions that may well inform the modern
readings of Pauline discourse.

The field of New Testament studies has often eschewed
theoretical considerations. Some would avoid theory on the
basis of its alleged irrelevancy, arguing that what is needed is
not theory but rather a commonsense approach to the text. In
other words, one ought not to impose external categories on the
text, but rather ought to allow the text's truth to speak. Such a
position depends upon a philosophy of language which presupposes a transparency of reference (that is, that language refers
in a simple and straightforward fashion to a self-evident field of
referents). Furthermore, this position seems naïvely unaware of
its own assumptions and categories. Not only are the relationships of text to theory, text to context, text to interpretation, far
more dynamic and complex than is allowed by this position; but
even this position is implicitly grounded in a theory of interpretation, though its presuppositions may remain unexamined by
those who espouse it.

There are also some critics who see theory as dangerous, as
a threat to the uniqueness of Christianity. They fear that using
theoretical language to talk about New Testament texts makes
early Christianity look like any other religious movement and its
texts look like any other texts. This is a danger I am willing to
court. Early Christianity can in fact be quite fruitfully engaged,

and to a degree explained, in terms of theories of social formation and language.

When theory has played a role in the interpretation of New
Testament texts or Christian origins, it has tended to do so in
two realms that rarely interact (though this lack of interaction
has been less by conscious design than by the tastes and interests of the researchers engaged in the practice). These two
realms are literary theory and social theory. A variety of helpful
studies have been produced or are currently applying the tools
from these two theoretical realms to the field of New Testament
studies. Literary studies tend to focus on patterns of representation and various forms of audience analysis, trying to take into
account how a text might be received and the variations among
audiences. Sociological studies, on the other hand, tend to use
the text for what it can reveal about the culture that produced
it and tend not to read the texts as literary objects.

Positioned in the space between these two types of scholarly
investigation, this present study acknowledges that both social
forms and the discourses that construct and sustain them are
central to the creation of new social meanings (cf. the theoretical position of Mack 1987). When I read the New Testament, I
see a complex struggle taking place over social forms and
meanings. A new interpretation of power is being produced,
located in a matrix of emerging social relations and articulated
through self-referential claims to authority. This work questions
how early Christian language and social organization are tied to
early Christian *ideas* about texts and social formations. In other
words, how are modes of organizing social life bound up with
the production of texts that explain them? Such an investigation
requires a dual focus on what is said and what is not said about
this relationship. In what follows, I will outline the theoretical
framework of this study, summarizing those dimensions of
Foucault's work on power and the articulation of truth that
have been significant for my own thinking about Paul's discourses of power.

It is perhaps misleading to speak of Foucault's work on
power as theory: Foucault himself set his analytics of power
explicitly over against theory, insofar as theory is meant to refer

to "a context-free, ahistorical, objective description" (Dreyfus and Rabinow 1982:184). Further, he is uneasy about the notion of theory because of a concern shared more broadly by most post-structuralist thinkers: that theory tends toward attempts to produce totalizing explanations, which risk both utopianism and imperialism (see Foucault 1977:231, 233; 1980e:78). Nevertheless, it is possible to construct for oneself a *theoretical position* from which to speak, grounded in Foucault's more general observations about the nature of power relations, a position from which to interpret a cultural artifact from a particular historical moment. In this case, the artifact is the corpus of the authentic Pauline epistles, the product of a fairly short and definable moment in the history of Christian discourse and practice.

Foucault is one of the pivotal thinkers in the intellectual movement that has come to be called post-structuralism. Straddling the lines that separate the traditional disciplines of history and philosophy, he has offered thorough and telling critiques of the ways in which the human sciences have created knowledge about "man" as well as strategies for thinking about power relations in modern society. Summarizing the central aspects of his work is a rather awesome task, one taken on at risk of being either foolishly simple-minded or hopelessly redundant. Many able secondary works exist already on the contributions of Foucault, and it is not my goal to replicate them.[1] Nevertheless, it is helpful to articulate a theoretical position shaped by Foucauldian insights before taking on the task of producing individual readings of the texts.

Foucault's work offers rich suggestions concerning the production of particular forms of truth as well as the practices of power that derive authority from the construction of "truth" and that lend authority to that process of construction. Foucault's studies focus on specific institutions and practices in Western culture where disciplinary knowledge shapes the human subject. While his *oeuvre* includes over 300 books, articles, interviews, reviews, and occasional pieces, I will concentrate on the most well known works here (see Bernauer and Keenan 1988 for a complete bibliography).

His analysis of the emergence of the modern subject in *The Order of Things* has challenged students of the human sciences to rethink both their subject matter and the tools they use to examine their data (Foucault 1966). His very use of the name "subject" for the modern individual is a play on the various significations associated with this word: one is a subject in the grammatical sense (as in the subject of a sentence), in the psychological sense (as possessing a unified identity), and in the political sense (as being subject to dominant powers). By demonstrating how Enlightenment categories invented the modern category, "man," he challenged by implication the methodological tools and assumptions contemporary students of culture have inherited from the 18th century. "Man" as a knowing subject and as the object of "scientific" knowledge is placed off-center. Foucault's critique of the Enlightenment episteme is particularly telling for biblical criticism, whose modern categories and practices were born of the Enlightenment's reorientation of thinking. While this reorientation made possible the crucial gesture of wrenching free "sacred scripture" from the realm of the divine, it also created a new fiction of transcendental power, located now in the free, autonomous, self-knowing human being (or more precisely, biblical critic).

An earlier study laid the groundwork for this critique of Enlightenment presuppositions and for later investigations into the ways in which the knowledge of "experts" creates social institutions for the management of deviance.[2] *Madness and Civilization* (1961) shows how this same Enlightenment that produced the thinking subject also produced a concept of madness against which sanity could be measured.

The Birth of the Clinic (1972) traces the history of the emergence of the hospital as the authorized site for the infirm. At this site, the clinical experts record the symptoms and treatments of the sick, place them in orderly physical arrangements, and create a notion of the "healthy" in contrast to an emerging image of the ill.

Discipline and Punish (1975) further investigates technologies of domination through knowledge. As experts collect and arrange knowledge about the criminally deviant, they also create the category of the criminal. Foucault demonstrates that knowledge of criminal behavior and assumptions about rehabilitation emerged at a particular point in history and resulted in the physical arrangement and ordering of the "deviant." Foucault narrates the transformation of the idea of appropriate treatment of the criminal from physical punishment to moral reformation, and the concomitant architectural and institutional practices that emerged from this shift.

The History of Sexuality (1976; 1984a; 1984b) begins to explore the connections between expert knowledge and technologies of power in the construction of human being as the possessor of a quality called "sexuality," and to examine various strategies for the policing of individual bodies and minds. Foucault argues that it was only in the nineteenth century that "sexuality" became an aspect of human personality. Prior to that, people performed sexual acts but they did not possess a "sexual identity." Once identity and sexual practice were linked, new concerns for social control of individual bodies and imaginations emerged, and the confessional was replaced by the analyst's couch.

In each of these works, the interconnectedness of dominant forms of knowledge with the creation of hierarchical and asymmetrical relations of power in societies remains a crucial concern for Foucault.

That Foucault focuses so much of his analysis on the construction of the "deviant" is no accident. For Foucault, the identification of the "other" is what enables the production of identity and the privileging of the "same." In one critic's words, otherness is "the historical a priori of Western culture, whether it appears in the guise of unreason or of the alien, strange, and incomprehensible" (Harootunian 1988:117). Foucault's understanding of the construction of the foil of the other as a cultural necessity in Western civilization is obviously telling in the context of this study of Paul's insistence on imitation—the valorization of sameness, or what Biddy Martin has called in another context, "the hegemony of the identical" (B. Martin 1988:13)— and his attempts to bracket all forms of difference as other or alien.

Foucault's lens is always trained on two objects that are co-creative: the object of study and the disciplinary tools deployed to study the object. Therefore, his critique oscillates between his subject matter and the disciplinary frame that gives that matter form and meaning. This doubled focus has been an important point of departure for the present work: my practice of reading Paul's texts differently from the ways in which they traditionally have been read is aimed both at a critique of traditional disciplinary practices and at producing a new reading of the subject matter of early Christian discourse and practice.

Foucault himself has stated that his research relates to notions that can be named simply, power and knowledge. Gaining access to the referents behind these names is a more difficult and often confounding process. "Power" in particular tends to be defined by Foucault primarily in terms of what he does not mean by it. This negative formulation is not fortuitous, but signifies rather a continual attempt on the part of Foucault to upset the conventional expectations of his audience. This audience's conceptions of power are indelibly stamped by the western European and later American liberal political traditions which describe power as a commodity held by some, desired by all, but set in trust with individuals and institutions through a political process. Foucault puts foward an alternative notion of power that removes from it this commodity status, this fetishized image of power. Power for Foucault is not a "thing" possessed by some people and withheld from others, but is a quality that inheres in relationships between people and groups of people:

> Power in the substantive sense, 'le' pouvoir, doesn't exist. What I mean is this. The idea that there is either located at— or emanating from—a given point something which is a 'power' seems to me to be based on a misguided analysis, one which at all events fails to account for a considerable number of phenomena. In reality, power means relations, a more-or-less organised, hierarchical, coordinated cluster of relations .
> . . . If one tries to erect a theory of power one will always be obliged to view it as emerging at a given place and time and hence to deduce it, to reconstruct its genesis. But if power is in reality an open, more-or-less coordinated (in the event, no doubt, ill-coordinated) cluster of relations, then the only

problem is to provide oneself with a grid of analysis which makes possible an analytic of relations of power. (Foucault 1980c:198-199)

Foucault's thinking about power appears primarily in his later writings, especially in his study of technologies of power emerging in the practice and rationalization of French penal systems. In *Discipline and Punish*, he offers the following statements about power:

> [P]ower exercised on the body is conceived not as a property, but as a strategy, . . . its effects of domination are attributed not to "appropriation", but to dispositions, manoeuvres, tactics, techniques, functionings; . . . one should decipher in it a network of relations, constantly in tension, in activity, rather than a privilege that one might possess; . . . one should take as its model a perpetual battle rather than a contract regulating a transaction or the conquest of a territory. In short this power is exercised rather than possessed; it is not the "privilege", acquired or preserved, of the dominant class, but the overall effect of its strategic positions—an effect that is manifested and sometimes extended by the position of those who are dominated. Furthermore, this power is not exercised simply as an obligation or a prohibition on those who "do not have it"; it invests them, is transmitted by them and through them; it exerts pressure upon them, just as they themselves, in their struggle against it, resist the grip it has on them. (Foucault 1979:26-27)

What is most suggestive for this inquiry is the notion that power is not a thing; rather power relations are ultimately coterminous with social relations. Power is not something one person or class holds over and against another person or class; rather, power constructs the contours of the relations between these, affecting both the dominator and the dominated. Commentators have called this aspect "self-formation or autocolonization" (Dreyfus and Rabinow 1982:186).

Power may be analyzed by tracing its practice, it may be read in the processes by which it is articulated, but it may not be pinned down as a thing in itself. We can understand power by observing its workings, but we cannot grasp it as an object apart from its role in social relationships. Power is what characterizes social relations, and conversely, all social relations are power relations. Power circulates within the social body, connecting members with one another. It finds its analogy more closely in the fluidity and omnipresence of blood than in the analogy of the brain, the site of command.[3] For contemporary political struggles organized around a utopian vision of freedom from power, Foucault's reformulation of an analytics of power has far-reaching implications, as Cousins and Hussain note (1984:230). Specifically, Foucault challenges the idea that an ideal social formation would be one in which power was not present, that social transformation has to do with liberation from power. These implications apply as well for the study of processes of power at different moments in history, particularly at moments when ideological transformations are taking place, or, put another way, when truth is being reformulated. For the emergence of new discourses of truth, there are also new assertions about power and new practices of power.

Whether in a historical setting or in contemporary liberation struggles, power inheres in the attempts at its own rearticulation; that is, it is not a situation of the *powerless* demanding the relinquishing of power by the *powerful*. Rather, it is a struggle over interpretations of power, conflicts over authority and truth. Such a reformulation of the concept of power does not deny that power relations can produce very ghastly deployments of brute force in real political struggles; however, it suggests that even the most coercive system is never absolute, never complete, but is engaged perennially in a struggle to put forward its singular truth. Alternative forms of truth are never completely eliminated, even when the most excessive coercions are present.

It is crucial to emphasize here the interactive character of power relations. All actors in a power relationship possess a critical access to agency. The ascendant figure in a power relationship does not act on the passive, subordinate figure. Although power relationships are asymmetrical, they do not render the subordinate actor without the possibility for action. Moreover, power is not coterminous with violence, Foucault would argue, though violence might be a practice deployed in a power relationship. Furthermore, power does not have to do with the presence or absence of consent. Foucault writes:

> A relationship of violence acts upon a body or upon things; it forces, it bends, it breaks on the wheel, it destroys, or it closes the door on all possibilities. Its opposite pole can only be passivity, and if it comes up against any resistance it has no other option but to try to minimize it. On the other hand a power relationship can only be articulated on the basis of two elements which are each indispensable if it is really to be a power relationship: that "the other" (the one over whom power is exercised) be thoroughly recognized and maintained to the very end as a person who acts; and that, faced with a relationship of power, a whole field of responses, reactions, results, and possible inventions may open up.
>
> . . . But even though consensus and violence are the instruments or the results, they do not constitute the principle or the basic nature of power . . . . In itself the exercise of power is not violence; nor is it a consent which, implicitly, is renewable. It is a total structure of actions brought to bear upon possible actions; . . . it is nevertheless always a way of acting upon an acting subject or acting subjects by virtue of their acting or being capable of action. (1982:219-220)

When I assert that New Testament texts represent interpretations of power and construct new forms of power relationships, I am not making an argument about force or consent. I am not, for example, arguing that certain texts construct social relations in accordance with or against the wills of the individuals in those early Christian communities. I agree with Foucault that the argument from will is beside the point. Rather, I would argue that the discourse of early Christian texts sets the terms in which questions of violence and will can be addressed. This is an explicit rejection of the schematized notion, most often set in opposition to liberalism's notion of the autonomous self, of the absolutely alienated subject who is the passive victim of ideology. The process is more complex than the simple production of "false consciousness," for example, and must be seen as a product of the agency of both poles of the power relationship.

There exists a danger in appropriating these notions from Foucault's studies, in that he is dealing specifically with a modern configuration of power and institutions. It is not self-evident that such categories transfer usefully to the context of the Hellenistic and Roman world. Nevertheless, there are several reasons for thinking that this attempt is justifiable.

First, the content of the texts being studied here deals with questions of social formation and social order. That is, these texts are concerned with establishing the boundaries of the group and maintaining order within the group itself, with disciplines of the body, with power relations and questions of authority. Second, the nascent attempts at normalization which are evident in the texts, and the ways in which discourse is deployed to rationalize that normalization, seem to follow the general pattern which Foucault describes. Third, although particular technologies of power are located by Foucault in modern centralized societies, they also more generally have to do with claims to self-evidency and truth. Just so, the Pauline discourses which construct the early power relations in the early communities are rationalized by claims to truth. Finally, it might be noted that the influence of Foucault here should be understood less as a literalist influence than an ironic one. That is, it is not possible to extract from Foucault's dense discourse any sort of clear-cut "sociological model" into which one might try to fit a particular set of ideological statements and social relations in order to prove something "true" about a particular social formation, in this case, early Christian communities. Rather, his contribution is what might be characterized as a kind of critical perspective that highlights the contingency of any sort of interpretive gesture.[4]

Foucault's observations about the nature of power relations and their relationship to truth claims are helpful in establishing a general corrective in the readings of Paul's use of the rhetoric of imitation. It is at this level that Foucault's influence on this study should be read.

For early Christianity which consciously articulated a new truth, a new interpretation of power, this realignment of the analytics of power relations invites us to read rather differently the assertions of power and truth found in the New Testament. Foucault sees in the emergence of Christianity less the radical change in the code of ethics with which Christianity is conventionally credited than the dispersal of new power relations. He calls this particular form of power "pastoral power," and he offers this schematization of it:

(1) It is a form of power whose ultimate aim is to assure individual salvation in the next world.

(2) Pastoral power is not merely a form of power which commands; it must also be prepared to sacrifice itself for the life and salvation of the flock. Therefore, it is different from royal power, which demands a sacrifice from its subjects to save the throne.

(3) It is a form of power which does not look after just the whole community, but each individual in particular, during its entire life.

(4) Finally, this form of power cannot be exercised without knowing the inside of people's minds, without exploring their souls, without making them reveal their innermost secrets. It implies a knowledge of the conscience and an ability to direct it.

This form of power is salvation oriented (as opposed to political power). It is oblative (as opposed to the principle of sovereignty); it is individualizing (as opposed to legal power); it is coextensive and continuous with life; it is linked with a production of truth—the truth of the individual himself. (Foucault 1982:214ff)

In New Testament writings, this form of pastoral power appears again and again. Foucault's observations about the specificity of Christian interpretations of power may be expanded and fruitfully set in relation to a series of notions that appear central to New Testament writings: the ideas of authoritative discourse, whether construed as "the words of the Lord," as the authoritative writing of the apostle Paul whose letters represent (him in) his absence, or as the Word of God ("the logos was made flesh"); of martyrdom as death and as witness (a telling) and as victory (an inversion of conventional power relations, repression becoming exaltation); of emerging institutions and practices that reinscribe the truth of Christian claims about power and truth. Power and its deployment are central topics in New Testament writings, whether cosmic (magical, possessing, exorcising, healing), social (bound up with obsessions over authority to speak and order communal existence), or individual (faith constructed as power).

From Foucault we gain a healthy suspicion of the "naturalness" of social forms and the truth claims that accompany them, as he documents again and again that the very organization of social life into institutions (where even architecture is not benign nor empty of power to construct meanings) serving social needs is itself a strategy of power. He teaches us by implication that the emerging institutions of early Christianity—*ekklēsia*, modeled on family, bound up with the language of sameness and identity—need to be interrogated for what they say about early Christian understandings of the circulation of power. They must not be explained as inevitable, pragmatic, or self-evident, but rather explored for what they can tell us about a crucial dimension of the unfolding of power relations in Western culture. That these power relations continue to be held up by the majority of the Christian West as self-evident or obvious is a testimony to the tenacity of Christian discourse in sustaining its particular interpretations of power. But we must remind ourselves continually of the constructed nature of this truth.

Foucault's analytic of power also offers a helpful insight by resisting notions of global/total power and by focusing instead on local forms of power (see Deleuze 1988:25ff). By bringing the exploration to the minutiae of strategies of power, the micro-technologies of power (in the prison, the confessional, or the nursery), he reminds us that power is exercised more often than not in quotidian, mundane ways: that bodies and populations are ordered and normalized through the micro-movements of the shaping of logics, more often than by brute force; that the subject is implicated just as the sovereign is, the prisoner and the jailer, the patient and the clinician. Each is constructed in relation to the other, through the operations of power, through agency. Again, this is not to assert that real forms of coercion do not exist, but that usual dynamics of power are not limited to nor coterminous with the concept of repression. Therefore, my focus here is on the minutiae of early Christian discourses, practices, and institutions—on the creation of the authority of the author and the speaker, on the policing of

Christian bodies and relationships, on the small and multifarious ways in which the Christian interpretations of truth and power came to take on universal dimensions, "naturalness," and to produce within Christian social institutions a regime of truth.

Early Christianity may be thought of as an emerging regime of truth. This regime of truth, along with practices of policing bodies and ordering populations and rationalizing these practices through a discourse of self-identical truths, moves over time and through the minutiae of dominating practices toward an ever more imbedded matrix of belief, convincing itself more and more of its own universal status. Part of this process is tied to the crucial problem in early Christianity of who speaks and who does not. Foucault reminds us at one point that what is said is not as important as who speaks.[5]

For early Christian discourse, the problem of authoritative discourse is worked out in a number of rhetorical and material ways. In the New Testament in general one sees the rhetorical force of certain speaking subjects, be they the veiled narrators of gospel stories or the foregrounded image of the apostle emerging from the epistles. In the very collection of these texts into a book called "the New Testament," one sees a clear strategy of power. The question of who speaks and who does not is resolved by the process of collection and delineation of authoritative discourse. The texts we call "the New Testament" are collected under the sign of "canon," a term oscillating between self-authorization (partly through its etymological link to juridical forms of truth), and the concomitant de-authorizing of alternative knowledges which are more or less systematically degraded, debased, and eventually all but completely destroyed in the creation of the authoritative text. While this book does not deal specifically with the issue of canonicity, it is nevertheless important to point out that the subject matter and its organization into a corpus included in an authoritative book is itself a strategic and interpretive move.

It was not until quite late in Foucault's career that he set out a clearly articulated plan for analyzing power relations, though the points he eventually outlined as important for that analysis are implicit in his earlier works (Foucault 1982:223). Each point contributes to or enables the creation and sustenance of power relations.

(1) One must be able to define the *system of differentiations* which allows the person or group in the dominant position in the hierarchical relationship to act upon the actions of the person or group in the subordinate position. In other words, there must be an underlying ideology of difference which creates "self" and "other" in the relationship, along with all the other oppositions that enable the social system to function.

(2) The *types of objectives* held by those who act upon the actions of others must be articulated. One might use here the language of desire and characterize power relations as a series of conflicting desires, borne out through struggle.

(3) There must be an identifiable *means* for bringing these relationships into being. Social structures and networks provide the possibility for desires to meet and conflict, and for the agents within power relations to engage one another.

(4) The fourth essential feature of an analysis of power relations is the identification of the *forms of institutionalization* of power. Power circulates within social networks, but passes through structures where it is concentrated, defined, and deployed: these structures are social institutions. Foucault has analyzed institutions such as prisons and hospitals, and for the study of the New Testament, the institution is the *ekklêsia*, the church. While it has been established that no unified institution called *ekklêsia* yet existed, the image of a unified institution is present as an emerging and singular *ideal* in New Testament texts.

(5) The final point to be analyzed in relation to power relations is the *degree of rationalization* of power relations. The processes by which power relations are rendered obvious and natural are crucially important to an analysis of power. It is here more than anywhere else that the relationship between power and knowledge is foregrounded, as power relations are rationalized discursively as representing a larger truth.

These steps are not necessarily sequentially arranged. The fifth point, for example, circles back to reinforce the first. Yet each element must be analyzed in order to understand the mechanisms of power.

As we rethink early Christianity, Foucault's analytics of power offer a way of integrating the analysis of a range of discursive formations—texts and institutions—in the production of new interpretations of truth. Foucault's analyses of technologies of power in various Western social formations provide a model for my own analysis of the ways in which what was once culturally scandalous became eventually normative and self-evident. This process was not unidirectional, nor was it imposed from on high. The strategies of power that produced the eventual cultural victory of Christianity are far more complex and multi-leveled than that; this book aims at suggesting some ways in which the process began.

For clarity's sake, what follows is a quite schematic set of definitions of the language used throughout this study. Abstract language is often characteristic of post-structuralist texts, and appears often to those unfamiliar with it to function primarily as jargon, obfuscating meaning rather than enabling it. While I find the technical language often helpful in its nuances, I am anxious to avoid unnecessary confusion.

DEFINITIONS

Power and the Political

It is assumed that the construction of power relations in any set of social networks is a complex process involving more than one set of factors. In this study, the discursive and ideological factors which contribute to the construction of power relations will be the focus, primarily because they are the factors most available given the nature of the evidence for early Christian social formations in this period. Other traditional arenas for the construction of power relations—the realms of economic, military, and political/state power relations—are not particularly relevant for the study of earliest Christian social networks because of their marginal status in the face of dominant and hegemonic power relations (the Roman empire). It is precisely because of this marginal status that the discursive and ideological factors for constructing power relations became so important in the first centuries of Christian practice. Other forms of power were inaccessible, and ideological power became the single possible mode of articulating a powerful and compelling stance.[6]

The most important aspects of ideology in its contribution to the construction of power relations are its claims to truth and its drive to produce an all-encompassing, singular, and "natural" truth.[7] This parallels the drive of social networks toward institutionalization, which is a kind of structural truth. In the Christian setting, the claim to truth and the drive toward a singular and natural version of that truth can be seen working throughout the discursive expressions of the earliest writers, most notably Paul, and in the institutionalizing gestures that occur from almost the very start. It is reproduced mimetically in much of the scholarship on early Christianity, in many of the claims to self-evidence. The discussion of scholarly analyses of Paul's own discourses (chapter four) will examine some of these claims.

Power in this study is understood as a fluid and relational force that permeates and cirulates within the social body. Power is coterminous with social relations in general. It is presumed that the very nature of power relations is that they are nonegalitarian and asymmetrical (Dreyfus and Rabinow 1982:185). Power relations are undergirded and sustained in a variety of complex ways, and in this study, the discursive and ideological factors which contribute to the establishment of power relations in early Christian communities will be the focus of discussion. This does not mean that these discursive and ideological factors are the *only* source of power relations, but they are the most significant in this moment in Christian history.

A final note concerning the use of language about power relations in this study, and that is the use of the adjective, "political." I use this term as the adjectival form of "power" itself, not to refer to more conventional referents such as the political process, the state, and so on. In this usage, "political" should be understood to imply a general sense of the ability to persuade and coerce—here, not through threats of physical harm, but in the realm of ideology, through equally coercive threats to one's access to salvation. It also marks a certain lack of innocence in the use of language. When I say that a particular commentator has ignored the political aspect of a passage in Paul's letters, I mean that he has neglected to account for the powerful nature of the Pauline discourse itself—its ability to persuade because of the implicit threat of deprivation (of salvation) that exists there.

Discourse and Rhetoric

The terms "discourse" and "rhetoric" appear frequently in this study, and their particularized usage should clarified. As with the theoretical aspects of power, "discourse" here is strongly influenced by Foucault's work on it.[8] The term "discourse" describes something greater than simple representation. It implies rhetoric cast in its broadest sense, of that which persuades and coerces, that which has a political motive—that is, a motive inscribed by power. Discourse is never innocent, it discloses the incapacity of any rhetoric to convey the truth. The use of the term "discourse" here is meant to evoke just this lack of innocence, the inability of any language to represent simply and disinterestedly. Discourse is an active constructor of ideology; it is through discourse that ideology makes its claims to truth. In this sense, discourse serves the social construction of power relations, and the matter of who speaks and who is silent takes on all the more importance.

Foucault's notion of *discursive formation* articulates the ideological force of discourse. A discursive formation comprises the full range or field of knowledge, formulated within the interaction of power and knowledge. Discourse and practice are tightly woven together in the notion of a discursive formation. What can be thought or known is constituted by power, which delimits the thought and the unthought.

> Thus a discursive formation unites thought and practice in a seamless and circular web: Practices set the conditions for discourse and discourse feeds back statements that will facilitate practice. Discourse appears completely incorporated into

practice. It has no autonomous identity or distance. (Wolin 1988:184)

When I use the term "rhetoric" in the interpretation of Paul's letters, I mean it in a broad, non-innocent way. I do not refer particularly to the influence of Greco-Roman schools of rhetoric upon his writing, though others have demonstrated the fruitfulness of such a comparison (Betz 1979; Stowers 1981). Rather, I refer to the more general rhetoricity of the text itself, its perspectival nature, its political tone. Such a usage is aimed at highlighting the contingent nature of Paul's discourse, at focusing the reader's attention on the ideological force of the text. The claim to truth which undergirds so much of Paul's discourse must be seen through this lens of the rhetorical nature of the text: it is a *claim* to truth, but not truth itself.

A further theoretical assumption of this study is that it matters very much that discourse and rhetoric originate from certain quarters, from the mouths and pens of particular speakers and writers, people who are imbued implicitly and explicitly with a kind of authority because of the inherently powerful nature of discourse itself. Foucault's examination of discourses that construct institutions (prisons, clinics, the confessional) always turns to the discourses of "the experts," those articulators of discourse who function as the speakers-who-are-supposed-to-know. In this singular description, I collapse the notions of power and knowledge within the authoritative figure of the speaker/writer. In the case of early Christian discourse, we know that the status of the discourses we have (and have not) is constructed through a combination of theological intentionality and historical accident, but we also know that the preservation of orthodox discourse is no historical accident. It can be assumed that Paul has been accorded the status of the speaker-who-is-supposed-to-know. The question of the relationship between authorship and authority, discursive expression and silence, is related to the question of the relationship between discourse and social formations, and will be discussed below. For the moment, it is important to note that the claim to encompassing truth embodied in ideological discourse is replicated in the structural realities of who speaks and who is silent.

Social Formation

"Social formation," "social networks" and similar language refer to the structural ways that early Christian groups began to organize themselves into communities. The language is meant to evoke a sense of fluidity because, although the process of institutionalization is a drive toward a unitary system, social groups and society in general are described better in terms of interaction, diffusion, and dynamism, and not in purely structural terms.[9] Therefore, the terminology, "social formation," is particularly evocative, because it implies movement rather than stasis, the social group in process of formation rather than the social group as always already institutionalized.

Throughout this work I will describe "early Christian social formations" with terms like "Christian discourse and practice" and "early Christian groups or communities"—rather than with terms such as "the early Church" or "early Christianity." This is a conscious attempt to create an image of diffusion and variety more appropriate to the discourse about early Christian activity. My rhetorical move is neither new nor particularly radical; the point has been made before, primarily in connection with the notions of "orthodoxy" and "heresy." Here, though, I am pressing the point at the level of discourse; that is, I want to suggest that "Christianity," in any sort of univocal or monolithic sense, is a later invention of discourse,[10] and that its reification is a move toward normalization and control. Just so, when discussing early Christian discourse—such as Paul's—one can identify certain nascent gestures toward the creation of "Christianity," gestures whose controversy (and therefore contingency) is demonstrated in the rhetorical fervor which envelop them. It remains an interesting—if unanswerable— question whether all speech acts performed by the-one-who-is-supposed-to-know display this tendency toward reification and normalization, or whether there exists a real alternative to the processes described and critiqued here.

The Relationship between Discourse and Social Formation

The relationship presupposed here between discourse and social formation is dialectical and interactive. Discourse is no simple reflection of social reality, but rather it performs a constructive role, creating the contours of social experience. There is no authentic social experience, per se; social relations and the ways one thinks about them are constructed by discourse: discourse "invents" social relations and is reinscribed by them. This is why the question of who speaks and who is silent—and the assignment of the role of privileged speaker—is so important to the whole question of how one views social formation in general and the particular relationship of early Christian discourse to early Christian social relations.

The discourse of the privileged speaker (Paul, for example) creates the contours of the social experience of early Christian communities. This is often worked out in struggle, as the ferocity of Paul's rhetoric at certain points makes clear. In the face of this struggle, the claim to truth on the part of the privileged speaker's discourse takes on more urgency and heightened rhetorical fervor. The drive toward truth takes two paths which are reflections of each other: the drive toward a singular Christian truth in the realm of correct teaching, and the drive toward a unitary structural truth in the guise of institutionalization. In both cases, the discursive strategy is to make the truth singular, all-encompassing, and natural. The diffusion and specificity of the social groups that called themselves Christians are replaced by a singularity of purpose and a universalism, both of which undercut and indict particularity and difference.

The Meaning of Imitation as a Discourse of Power in Paul's Letters

Within this theoretical frame, what does it mean, then, to assert that Paul's letters deploy the notion of imitation "as a discourse of power"? What is the sense of the ambiguous genitive? Should it be read as a genitive of possession? Is "imitation," then, "power's discourse," the very articulation of power? Or perhaps it could be read as a genitive of respect: "imitation" as a way of articulating power relations and claiming for them a grounding in truth. I see it as both of these, and perhaps even more diffuse than just these two possibilities. My reading appears as mobile and heterologous, oscillating between possible meanings on this hinge of grammatical ambiguity. This reading attempts to resist the arrogant singularity of the drive toward truth, recognizing its elusive and contingent status. It seeks to describe a certain moment in a particular discourse—Paul's deployment of the notion of imitation in his letters to early Christian communities—as just one particularly poignant sign of the more general drive toward singularity, sameness, and truth in much Christian discourse. The poignancy derives from the repetition involved: the discourse of imitation, articulated by the privileged speaker-who-is-supposed-to-know and producing a particular set of power relations based on an economy of sameness, and the very function of imitation itself point to this drive toward truth. The dialectical quality of discourse and social relations could have no better representation than in Paul's discourse of imitation and its rhetorical effects on the power relations of early Christian communities.

THE USEFULNESS OF FOUCAULT

To conclude, then, I want to emphasize that my use of Foucault to read Paul's rhetoric of imitation is a strategic one. In appropriating some crucial concepts from Foucault's highly complex work, I have certainly not done justice to his extremely difficult, often confounding, and sometimes elusive thought. Further, I have purposefully bracketed some of the interesting interventions into and critiques of his work produced by thinkers of a variety of political positions and philosophical bents (but see Arac 1988; Diamond and Quinby 1988; Fraser 1989; Hoy 1980, among others). I am not suggesting that these interventions and critiques are not important, but I have limited my use of Foucault's analytics to a strategic one. That is, in pursuing a "Foucauldian reading" of Paul, my purpose was not to demonstrate a privileged truthfulness to Foucault's perspective, nor to produce a totalized new reading of Paul. Rather, I have attempted to imagine what a reading-otherwise might look like, and Foucault is a congenial if sometimes erratic partner in such a project. His intellectual role has been likened somewhat playfully by feminist philosopher Nancy Fraser, following critic Susan Sontag, to that of a lover from whom women tolerate styles different from what they expect of husbands. Fraser calls Foucault "unrecuperable," and then quotes Susan Sontag:

> Great writers are either husbands or lovers. Some writers supply the solid virtues of a husband: reliability, intelligibility, generosity, decency. There are other writers in whom one prizes the gifts of a lover, gifts of temperament rather than moral goodness. Notoriously, women tolerate qualities in a lover—moodiness, selfishness, unreliability, brutality—that they would never countenance in a husband, in return for excitement, an infusion of intense feeling. In the same way, readers put up with unintelligibility, obsessiveness, painful truths, lies, bad grammar—if, in compensation, the writer allows them to savor rare emotions and dangerous sensations. And, as in life, so in art both are necessary, husbands and lovers. It's a great pity when one is forced to choose between them. (Sontag 1966:52, cited in Fraser 1989:65)

I, too, cite this text playfully, not of course to invite the accusation of "immorality" upon the project, but to underscore the challenge of Foucault's ways of seeing, a challenge that in my judgment reinscribes the project with pleasure and excitement. As Nancy Fraser has put it:

> Foucault, one might conclude, isn't much good as a husband . . . . . But he makes a very interesting lover indeed. His very outrageousness in refusing standard humanist virtues, narrative conventions, and political categories provides just the jolt we occasionally need to dereify our usual patterns of self-interpretation and renew our sense that, just possibly, they may not tell the whole story. (Fraser 1989:65-66)

In my judgment, it is precisely this kind of jolt that biblical criticism can use, and to quite good advantage.

3

THE FRAME OF
REFERENCE:
DISCOURSES
OF
MIMESIS
IN
ANTIQUITY

Ancient discourses of mimesis present a complex weave of images and analogies, and derive from a variety of ideological perspectives. In describing and interpreting these discourses, I do not seek to produce a univocal definition of mimesis as the monolithic background for studying imitation in Pauline discourse. If a single diachronic characteristic of mimesis exists, it is that it evades precise definition and reduction. In what follows, I will examine how mimesis functions within the variety of discourses in which it is found, seeking out commonalities and diversions in these functions, and attempting finally to extract some general conclusions about the ways in which mimesis was deployed in ancient writing and practice.

ETYMOLOGY

Discussion of the origin of the Greek *mimēsis* word group has been largely inconclusive or highly speculative.[1] For example, the earliest attestations of the word group are relatively late, from the fifth century BCE. Most scholars conclude, therefore, that the word group was imported, although the original provenance of the term is far from certain. In his classic study of mimesis in antiquity, Hans Koller (1954:37-48) argues that the word group must have come to Greece with the arrival of the Dionysiac cult. Gerald Else, who challenges Koller's entire thesis, claims instead a Doric origin, from Sicily (Else 1958:78-79). Given, however, the scant evidence available, this debate cannot be adequately resolved. In any case, the question of origins has little significance for this present inquiry. Of more significance is how mimesis vocabulary became established in Greek usage, and what nuances of meaning it came to possess.

EARLIEST USAGES

Koller's study of the mimesis word group observes that many of its earliest occurrences are in contexts where music and dance are dominant themes. He concludes that the word-group cannot have signified "imitation" in any ordinary sense (*Nachahmung*) but rather "representation" (*Darstellung*) and "expression" (*Ausdruck*) (Koller 1954:12-13; 37-48). Koller's thesis is summarized in this way:

> . . . The point of departure for our work was the notion of mimesis in Aristotelian poetics. It occasioned for us an extensive examination of all of the generally available evidence for mimesis. This revealed that *mimêsis can* mean "imitation" but that the word also possesses in addition a whole range of meaning apart from the term "imitation" (*imitatio*). *Its central meaning lies in dance. Mimeisthai* primarily means "to bring to expression through dance." Bound up together with Greek dance was always rhythm, musical retinues, and storytelling. The observation that *mimos* and all the notions deriving from it came only from the sphere of cultic practice, and indeed from orgiastic cultus originally; further the data that it is not found in the earliest literary language despite the metrical suitability; and not permitting a connection with Indo-Germanic languages all lead us to the *presumption* that *mimos* designates the actor or the masker of dionysiac cult-drama. Independent of this illuminating research, it is however certain that *mimeisthai* means a representation in dance and that its wider

usages have evolved from this meaning . . . . (Koller 1954: 119; my translation)

Koller's thesis is supported by his interpretations of a number of ancient fragments which use the terms *mimos* and *mimeisthai* in festival contexts. The most important of these early attestations of *mimeisthai* as a cultic term is a fifth-century fragment of Aeschylus which describes a Dionysiac rite:

> . . . One, holding in his hands the pipe, the labour of the lathe, blows forth his fingered tune, even the sound that wakes to frenzy. Another, with brass-bound cymbals, raises a clang . . . the twang shrills; and unseen, unknown, bull-voiced mimes (*mimoi*) in answer bellow fearfully, while the timbrel's echo, like that of subterranean thunder, rolls along inspiring a mighty terror. (Nauck 1964:Fr. 57; Strab. *Geog.* 10.3.16)

Koller (1954:39) argues that the mimes described in this fragment actually hold a cultic office. It is not at all clear that the fragment supports such a conclusion. On the other hand, the conclusion is not necessary to sustain the more modest assertion that mimes perform a cultic *function* here and in general archaic cultic practice. That is, despite the fact that the attestations of the term *mimos* are extremely rare, especially in the pre-Socratic period, one could nevertheless make certain observations about the function of the mime in the cult.[2] Specifically, one could well argue with Koller that the *mimoi* provide the verisimilitude of the bull sound in the rite without elevating the mime to a ritual *office*. In addition, this early text has drawn together the important elements of the Dionysiac ritual with music and dance, and with the important participation of those who provide a mimetic representation of the voice of the bull (that is, the voice of the god).

This representational setting for the earliest attestations of the mimesis word-group is significant because of the close ties between dance, ritual expression, and the eventual development of theater in Greece (see Reich 1903). One might well imagine the process of mimesis in this context as a continuum. At one end a rite is performed as a mimetic reminder of a particular incident in myth, and at the other end ritual action becomes, in the minds of participants and observers, an actual, repeated duplicate of the original action (Adrados 1975:270-277). In this context, there does not appear to be the kind of opposition between original and copy which becomes important from Plato on.

The incorporation of imitation into ritual practices is pervasive in the religions of Greco-Roman antiquity. Plutarch's description of Isis's incorporation of her sufferings into her rites is instructive on this point:

> . . . [T]he sister and wife of Osiris, after she had quenched and suppressed the madness and fury of Typhon, was not indifferent to the contests and struggles which she had endured, nor to her own wanderings nor to her manifold deeds of wisdom and many feats of bravery, nor would she accept oblivion and silence for them, but she intermingled in the most holy rites portrayals (*eikonas*) and suggestions (*huponoias*) and representations (*mimêmata*) of her experiences at that time, and sanctified them, both as a lesson in godliness and an encouragement for men and women who find themselves in the clutch of like calamities. (Plut., *De Is. et Os.* 27)

The goddess consciously constructs her own imitation into the rites which are dedicated to her. Further, the function of imitation here is twofold: first, as a "lesson in godliness," a theological reason, and second, as "an encouragement," a more mundane purpose.[3]

AESTHETIC MIMESIS

Many discussions of mimesis in antiquity tend to focus on Plato's notorious banishment of the poets from his ideal city in Book 10 of the *Republic*.[4] The debates concerning Plato's meaning fill volumes, and it is beyond the scope and interest of this study to pursue the details of these debates. Nevertheless, it is worth noting that much of the debate centers on whether or not Plato contradicts himself in his use of the term *mimêsis* (Greene 1918; Tate 1928; 1932; Havelock 1963). Among Plato scholars, only McKeon entertains the possibility that Plato uses a diversity of meaning. He states his position, in opposition to both Greene and Tate, as follows:

The word "imitation," as Plato uses it, is at no time established in a literal meaning or delimited to a specific subject
matter. It is sometimes used to differentiate some human
activities from others or some part of them from another part
or some aspect of a single act from another; it is sometimes
used in a broader sense to include all human activities; it is
sometimes applied even more broadly to all processes—human, natural, cosmic, and divine. Like most of the terms that
figure prominently in the dialogues, "imitation" as a term is
left universal in scope and indeterminate in application. The
dialectical method is used to determine its meaning in particular context, sometimes bringing out a meaning according to
which any given statement in which it may occur is true,
sometimes with equal force the meanings in which the statement is false; not infrequently both ends are accomplished in
a single dialogue. (1936:3-4)

In discussing aesthetic mimesis in Plato, what becomes clear
is that there is something else at stake besides the question of
whether imitation itself is good or bad. The problem is imitation's relationship to knowledge and to truth. In Book 10 of the
Republic, the painter and the tragedian are both indicted as
imitators who, in their nature as imitators, are thrice removed
from truth.[5] A little further on, Socrates calls the painter's
imitation deceitful and far removed from truth, because it "lays
hold of only a small part of the object and that a phantom
(*eidólon*)" (Pl., *Resp.* 598B). In the discussion of poetic creation
that follows, Socrates argues that poets would not bother with
creating poetic imitations if they were able to create exemplars,
and that their inability to do the latter is connected with their
lack of knowledge of the truth.[6] Contrasting imitative practice
and the possession of real knowledge, Socrates invokes the
example of Homer, who was not able to educate people and
make them better, but possessed only the art of imitation and
not real knowledge (Pl., *Resp.* 600C).

   This contrast between mimesis and real knowledge, or
access to the truth, is a persistent theme in the Platonic dialogues.[7] It is also an ironic theme, given the very nature of the
Platonic discourses which are completely mimetic in their
execution. The dialogues can hardly be characterized as the

"thought of Plato"; rather, the dialogues re-present Socratic discourse. Plato's account of Socrates's speech is a mimetic rendering of his mentor's articulations. So, while one finds throughout the Platonic texts indictments of mimetic activity, activity which inscribes the hierarchical separation between the privileged model (reality) and the derivative copy (art and poetry), it is also the case that Plato's writing—as with the artist's rendering or the poet's verse—attempts to mask its mimetic quality by making ultimate claims to truth. This observation must, at the very least, relativize the impact of the Socratic/Platonic condemnation of mimetic activity.[8]

Aristotle takes up the question of aesthetic mimesis in his *Poetics*, but he does not share the Platonic suspicion of the mimetic aspect of art. Rather, he grounds the origins of poetry in human nature's tendency toward imitation and in the pleasure which humans gain from representation:

> Speaking generally, poetry seems to owe its origin to two particular causes, both natural. From childhood people have an instinct for representation (*to te gar mimeisthai sumphuton tois anthrôpois ek paidôn esti*), and in this respect human beings differ from the other animals in that they are far more imitative and learn their first lessons by representing (*mimê-masi*) things. And then there is the enjoyment people always get from representations. What happens in actual experience proves this, for we enjoy looking at accurate likenesses of things which are themselves painful to see, obscene beasts, for instance, and corpses . . . . We have, then, a natural instinct for representation and for tune and rhythm—for metres are obviously sections of rhythms—and starting with these instincts humans very gradually developed them until they produced poetry out of their improvisations. (Arist., *Poet.* 1448B)

In the case of Aristotle, then, artistic imitation does not have the pejorative tenor attributed it by the Platonic dialogues. Indeed, mimesis is accorded the status of having derived from nature. It is a peculiarly human activity, and its offshoots (poetry and music) are natural outgrowths of human nature and instinct.

The power of artistic representation and imitation was not lost on those who discussed it in antiquity. In the *Laws* of Plato, for example, it is argued that musical imitation will have a significant impact on the souls of children, and that care in the performance of rhythms and harmonic compositions must be taken so as to turn the children toward the acquisition of virtue (Pl., *Leg.* VII, 812B-C; see also *Ti.* 19D-E). Only slaves and foreign hirelings, the text elsewhere argues, should be employed to perform mimicry of ludicrous comedy, and free men and women should never learn this kind of mime, lest their virtue be compromised (Pl., *Leg.* VII, 814-818). Several centuries later, the impact of the imitative arts on the formation of virtues was still very much a topic of discussion and debate, as Plutarch's defensive comments in his treatise, *How to Study Poetry*, would indicate (Plut., *Mor.* 14E-37B, esp. 17F-18F, 20B-C).

This brief overview indicates that the role of mimesis in artistic production and its concomitant ethical impact were recurrent and controversial themes in the artistic theory of antiquity. The Platonic emphasis on the relationship between imitation on the one hand and truth and knowledge on the other highlighted the derivative and hierarchical nature of mimesis. Others, notably Aristotle, tended not to be concerned in the same way with the model-copy relationship. Nevertheless, the Platonic conception became the dominant one in antiquity, Aristotle's later influence over discussions of mimesis notwithstanding. The power accorded mimetic representation to shape moral character contributed to this dominance. Plato's texts do not deny the power of imitation, but on the contrary, argue strongly against the mimetic practice of art especially because of the power of representation to transform ethics. In the Platonic economy, the danger of art lies precisely in that power: if imitation and representation are three steps away from truth, then the ethics which would derive from mimetic practice would also be divergent from the truth.

COSMOLOGICAL MIMESIS

In ancient literature, the relationship between the sensible world and the intelligible world is often described in mimetic language. The whole process of creation is explained in terms of universal models and earthly copies, and the notion of the individual and a microcosm is a very old one. While Democritus was the first to use the term itself (*en tô anthrôpô mikrô kosmô onti*),[9] probably toward the end of the fifth century, the notion of some kind of sympathetic relationship between heavenly bodies and earthly life was present in earlier astrological speculation (Cornford 1922/23:142, n. 4). Further, one finds in Pythagorean thought the assertion of a mimetic relationship between numbers and things.[10] Aristotle's *Metaphysics* is the source for this doctrine, specifically the famous sentence which seems to collapse any differences between Pythagorean cosmology and the Platonic theory of ideas:

> *tên de methexin tounoma metabalen [Platôn]· hoi men gar Pythagoreioi mimêsei ta onta phasin einai tôn arithmôn, Platôn de methexei, tounoma metabalôn.*
>
> Plato changed the name to participation; for the Pythagoreans said that things are in imitation of numbers, and Plato changed the word to participation. (Arist., *Metaph.* 987B)

The technical arguments surrounding this passage are largely beside the point for this discussion (but see Burkert 1972:43-45 for a summary). What is important to note here is that Aristotle, in attempting to collapse the two schools' theories, may well have had a rhetorical motive. He may have been trying to undermine the assertion that Plato's ideal doctrines were original (Burkert 1972:44). The result, then, would be to suggest that in pre-Socratic discourse a way of expressing a mimetic relationship existed quite apart from any idealism. Burkert demonstrates this possibility by citing two Hippocratic texts in which the relationship between the microcosm and the macrocosm is, in fact, a mimetic relationship, but there is no hierarchy involved. Burkert puts it this way:

> . . . [Aristotle] does say that the Pythagoreans supposed they saw *homoiômata* between things and numbers, and it is only natural to express such similarity or correspondence by the word *mimêsis*. Similarly, in the Hippocratic writings the relation of microcosm and macrocosm becomes a matter of "imitation," but—and here is the surprising fact—this imitation may be turned either way. One may just as well say that the human body "imitates" the cosmos as that the parts of the

cosmos "imitate" human organs. In the same way, either the arts imitate nature or nature imitates the arts. *Imitation is a two-sided correspondence, which makes it possible to interpret separate things following the same pattern, but without implying differences of rank or a relationship of ontological priority.* . . . When we place the Pythagorean theory in this pre-Socratic context, Aristotle's statement about "imitation" falls into place with the rest. *Nothing more is meant than the correspondence of cosmos and number, in the sense that one explains and illuminates the other.* In post-Platonic thought one can scarcely speak of imitation without assuming that it implies a gradation of kinds of Being, especially since Plato often characterizes the relation of sensible object and Idea as *mimêsis.* (Burkert 1972:44-45; emphasis mine)

Burkert's clarification of this separation between Pythagorean and Platonic cosmologies suggests that there existed a tradition of discourse about mimesis in which hierarchy was not necessarily operative. Nevertheless, Platonic discourse here, as elsewhere, functions as a kind of watershed. The notion of imitation is transformed in Plato's dialogues in such a way that one cannot appeal to mimesis without reference to the idealism and hierarchically structured ontology with which it is interwoven. Nowhere is the relationship between hierarchy and mimetic discourse clearer than in the cosmology outlined in Plato's *Timaeus.*[11]

One thing that becomes immediately clear from reading the *Timaeus* is that the dialogue presupposes the macrocosm-microcosm relationship and that it grounds human existence in an unchangeable, perfect and eternal foundation, that is, cosmic order. In producing the analogy of the individual soul and the universe's order, the dialogue offers a constant and absolute ethic:

> True morality is not a product of human evolution, still less the arbitrary enactment of human wills. It is an order and harmony of the soul; and the soul itself is a counterpart, in miniature, of the soul of the world, which has an everlasting order and harmony of its own, instituted by reason. (Cornford 1937:6)

While the visible world and the human beings within it are conceptualized in the *Timaeus* as analogies to the cosmic order, the difference between the model and the copy is also highlighted in the discourse and is embedded in the mimetic relationship itself. That is to say, there is always a nagging difference existing between the eternal model and the mortal copy. The mimetic relationship is motivated by the drive to erase that difference, to create sameness; but there will always be that unbridgeable gap between the model and the copy. This difference is articulated at the commencement of the *Timaeus*'s second explanation of creation, in which the notion of the Receptacle (Space) is introduced:

> We must, however, in beginning our fresh account of the Universe make more distinctions than we did before; for whereas then we distinguished two Forms, we must now declare another third kind. For our former exposition those two were sufficient, one of them being assumed as a Model Form, intelligible and ever uniformly existent, and the second as the model's Copy, subject to becoming and visible. (Pl., *Ti.* 48E)

One of the most striking expressions of the gap between and concomitant hierarchy of model and copy appears in the *Timaeus*'s discussion of the demiurge's position in the cosmic plan and its later work in creation. The model is attributed perfection, wholeness, and an idealized status, while the copy is a mere reflection and shadow of the model:

> When the father and creator saw the creature which he had made moving and living, the created image of the eternal gods, he rejoiced, and in his joy determined to make the copy still more like the original, and as this was an eternal living being, he sought to make the universe eternal, so far as might be. Now the nature of the ideal being was everlasting, but to bestow this attribute in its fullness upon a creature was impossible. Wherefore he resolved to have a moving image of eternity, and when he set in order the heaven, he made this image eternal but moving according to number, while eternity itself rests in unity, and this image we call time . . . . These are the forms of time, which imitates eternity

and revolves according to a law of number. (Pl., *Ti.* 37C-38B)

The universe, then, is understood to function as a created image of divinity, and by implication, to possess a derivative status.[12] Likewise, time is a derivative of eternity, an imitation but less full rendering of eternity and its characteristic unity.

When this creative principle, the demiurge, delegates creative power to the gods, this power is described as an imitation of the demiurge's own activity:

> Three tribes of mortal beings remain to be created . . . . [I]f they were created by me and received life at my hands, they would be on an equality with the gods. In order then that they may be mortal, and that this universe may be truly universal, do ye, according to your natures, betake yourselves to the formation of animals, imitating the power which was shown by men in creating you. The part of them worthy of the name immortal, which is called divine and is the guiding principle of those who are willing to follow justice and you—of that divine part I will myself sow the seed . . . . (Pl., *Ti.* 41B-C; see also 42E)

This passage suggests several characteristics of the mimetic relationship. First of all, mimetic activity is by its very nature derivative. That is, each level of being derives from the level preceding it; it imitates that level, and strives to attain to its level of perfection, but does not and cannot. If this were not the case, then the creative activity of the gods would have the same impact as that of the demiurge; that is, what the gods create would possess immortality.

The second important point this passage makes is that the gods' creative work has two goals. The first is to create animals which are mortal. The second is to assure through this creation that "this universe may be truly universal," that is, that the universe will be complete, will possess its true character. The universe's access to its own true character is tied to mimetic behavior on the part of the gods. Without this mimesis, the universe would be imperfect.[13]

The final point, though mentioned before, bears emphasis: an implicit hierarchy exists in the notion of mimesis invoked in this passage of the *Timaeus* and throughout the work. The demiurge has been modelled on the eternal being who is not born and who is apprehended only through reason (Pl., *Ti.* 27B, 31D), and the gods imitate the demiurge. Because of the divine particle inhabiting animals who, through following justice and the gods, might gain access to immortality, those creatures occupy a level in the hierarchy just below the gods.[14]

In this mimetic economy, human beings are understood to be imitators of divine proportions, heavenly shapes, and planetary movement and activity. Thus, the human head is round in imitation of the spherical shape of the universe; additionally, the head is the locus of the divine aspect of the human and functions as lord over the rest of the body (Pl., *Ti.* 44D). Sexual identity and reproductive function are noted as particularly imitative of universal forms. In the *Symposium*, Plato describes the origins of the sexes:

> The three sexes, I may say, arose as follows. The males were descended from the Sun, the females from the Earth, and the hermaphrodites from the Moon, which partakes of either sex, and they were round and they *went* round, because they took after their parents (*dia to tois goneusin omoia einai*). (Pl., *Symp.* 190B)

In the *Statesman*, reproduction is singled out as a special activity which had to change when the universe underwent change:

> Following the change in the universe, all other things had to change, and, in particular, a new law governing conception, birth, and nurture was made binding on the whole universe— and therefore on all creatures, for they must needs imitate its ways. (Pl., *Plt.* 274A)

Finally, in *Menexenus*, Plato notes: "Earth does not imitate woman in being pregnant and giving birth, but rather woman imitates the earth" (Pl., *Menex.* 238A).

In this conception of cosmic mimesis, the universe and its creatures are inextricably bound in a complex economy of sameness—a sameness which renders the universe possible and which provides it with its characteristic perfection. The hierarchy implied in the *Timaeus* creation myth implicates mimesis in its ordering, as one function which is activated by and sustains the system itself. Mimesis is essential to the creation myth and to the hierarchical relationship between the universe and the world, between the divine and the human, between ideality and reality. It motivates and undergirds the complex orderliness of the universe.

A similar set of notions can be found in the writings of Philo, who was clearly influenced by Platonic thought. One example will suffice to demonstrate how the notion of mimesis worked its way into Philo's thinking about creation. In his work, *On the Creation of the World*, one finds this statement:

> For God, being God, assumed that a beautiful copy (*mimêma*) would never be produced apart from a beautiful pattern (*paradeigma*), and that no object of perception would be faultless which was not made in the likeness of an original discerned only by the intellect. So when He willed to create this visible world He first fully formed the intelligible world, in order that He might have the use of a pattern wholly God-like and incorporeal in producing the material world, as a later creation, the very image of an earlier, to embrace in itself objects of perception of as many kinds as the other contained objects of intelligence. (Philo, *Op. Mund.* 16)

Here in Philo one finds the same ruling ideas about imitation and the relationship of the model to the copy. The intelligible world is the incorporeal and divine model for the material world, which strives to become like the intelligible. The tension between the drive toward sameness and nondifference on the one hand, and the inherent and necessary difference which separates model and copy on the other hand, reigns in Philo as in Plato.[15]

THE IMITATION OF GOD

Closely related to cosmological mimesis is the idea of the imitation of God (Crouzel 1978; Gulin 1925; Heitmann 1940; Merki 1952; Rutenber 1946). In Graeco-Roman antiquity, the constellation of ideas—to follow God (*epesthai theō, sunakolouthein tō theō*), to assimilate to God (*homoiōsis theō*), to imitate God (*mimeisthai, apomimeisthai*)—exhibits a unique and persistent hold on religious thought across several centuries.

The earliest evidence for this doctrine of human imitation of the divine shows the notion's importance for Pythagorean thought. While no evidence contemporaneous with earliest Pythagoreanism survives, all the credible sources from later periods suggest the importance of the imitation of God for the school. Arius Didymus, preserved in Stobaeus, ascribes the doctrine of *hepou theô* to Pythagoras (Stob., *Ecl.* 2.7.36).[16] Aelian in his history makes this statement about Pythagorean doctrine:

> *Pythagoras elege duo tauta ek tôn theôn tois anthôpois dedosthai kallista, to te aletheuein kai euergetein. kai prosetithei, hoti kai eoike tois theois ekateron.*
>
> Pythagoras said that the two best gifts of the gods to men were speaking the truth and showing kindness, and he added that both resembled works of the gods. (Ael., *VH* 12.59)

One of the most thoroughgoing sources for Pythagorean doctrine, Iamblichus's biography of Pythagoras, places the imitation of God at the center of Pythagorean ethics:

> All their decisions with regard to actions to be performed and to be avoided are directed towards agreement with the Divine: this is the first principle and their entire life is directed to following God (*ho bios apas suntetaktai pros to akolouthein tô theô*). The meaning of this philosophy is that a person acts in a ridiculous fashion when seeking the good elsewhere than with the gods: just as if a person in a country ruled by a king were to honor one of the citizens as a governor neglecting the ruler of the country as a whole. This is how they think that people in fact behave. (Iambl., *VP* 137 [= 86-87])

Earlier in Iamblichus's work (37-39), a related notion is developed, in which Pythagoras exhorts his listeners to assign privilege and authority to things and beings which are earlier or older. In the course of this discussion, which Iamblichus says was a way of urging people to consider their parents their betters, Pythagoras sets up an interesting hierarchy of value and obligation. Just as the leaders and founders of colonies are those most deserving of respect, he claims, so the gods are more deserving than dæmons (*daimones*), dæmons more so than demigods, heroes more than ordinary people, and finally, those who were the cause of birth above the young (37).

The connection with the imitation of God is not immediately apparent until one looks to other points in the tradition which make the connection explicitly.[17] A much earlier text, Plato's *Laws* (716B-718A), articulates this very same hierarchy in a section which discusses the wise person's desire to follow the steps of God, just as like is drawn to like. The text reads, "Every man ought so to devise as to be of the number of those who follow in the steps of the God (*hôs tôn xunakolouthêsontôn esomenon tô theô dei dianoêthênai panta andra*)." This is followed by a description of the behavior which is demanded of such a wise person who would attempt to follow God:

> He, then, that is to become dear to such a one [God] must needs become, so far as he possibly can, of a like character;
> . . . he amongst us that is temperate is dear to God, since he is like him (*ho men sophrôn hêmôn theô philos, homoios gar*), while he that is not temperate is unlike and at enmity (*ho de mê sophrôn anomoios te kai diaphoros kai adikos*). (Pl., *Leg.* 716C-D)

The discussion then turns to the pious acts demanded of the wise person, who will offer worship and honor, first to the Olympian gods and those of the underworld, then to the dæmons, and then to the heroes. Following these come ancestral deities, after which honor should be given to living parents. One can infer that attempting to follow God demands, almost contradictorily, that one take one's place in the hierarchy of honor and value: imitation and following of God are intricately bound up with ideas about proper place and appropriate value.

Perhaps the most important text in the Platonic corpus concerning the imitation of God is found in *Theaetetus* 176A-B. Here the characteristic Platonic dualism is inscribed as a necessary component of being on earth, and the only alternative which is presented is that of escape:

But it is impossible that evils should be done away with, Theodorus, for there must always be something opposed to the good; and they cannot have their place among the gods, but must inevitably hover about mortal nature and this earth. Therefore, we ought to try to escape from earth to the dwelling of the gods as quickly as we can; and to escape is to become like God, so far as this is possible (*phugê de homoiôsis theô kata to dunaton*); and to become like God is to become righteous and holy and wise (*dikaion kai hosion meta phrônêseôs*).

The rewards for becoming like God—righteousness, holiness, and wisdom—are especially available to the philosopher who, according to Plato, is the privileged imitator of God (Rutenber 1946:58-61, 86). The soul of the philosopher, as the most able follower of God, is located at the top of the human ontological hierarchy, while the rungs below are occupied in descending order by the souls of kings, politicians, doctors, prophets, poets, craftspeople, sophists and tyrants (Pl., *Phdr.* 248D-E). Rutenber puts special emphasis on the hierarchical nature of the imitation of God by philosophers and nonphilosophers:

The philosopher can take God as his model because he knows God. But the non-philosopher must follow God as he sees him in others. For him, the power of example is very great and he is enjoined, therefore, to look up to those more godlike than himself, and to follow them (*Leg.* 732A-B). (Rutenber 1946: 86)

Similar sentiments can be found throughout the Platonic corpus, in which the mimetic relationship is mediated through a hierarchical arrangement (see, for example, Pl., *Resp.* 389).

It is important to emphasize that the Platonic doctrine of the imitation of God is intertwined with the Platonic doctrine of forms (see Rutenber 1946: chapter 3). That is, the philosopher's relationship to God is like the relationship of the created world to the intelligible world. Just as the created world can only tend toward resemblance to the intelligible world, the philosopher does not have access to divinity but only to a likeness of divinity (Pl., *Phdr.* 278D). The form (God) is the limit to which one strives but never is able to attain. Likewise, those who imitate the philosophers will not become philosophers themselves, but will attain a position as like as possible.[18] The point cannot be made strongly enough: there exists in the notion of imitation this tension between the drive to sameness and the inability to achieve it, an inability which creates hierarchy.

Pythagoras and Plato were not the only philosophers to articulate doctrines of the imitation of God. The Epicurean school also conceived of a mimetic relationship between the gods and sages (Frischer 1982:78-79, 125-126; Frischer 1975: 212 n. 100; Merki 1952:7 n. 2; Schmid 1951). The hierarchical aspect which one finds in the Platonic discourse and which influences early Christian discourse is, however, largely absent from the Epicurean conception of deosimilitude. That is, in the Epicurean understanding, the sage has the opportunity to undergo apotheosis, at some extraordinary or exceptional moment when the sage achieves a level of perfection of ataraxy (Frischer 1982:78-79). Nevertheless, while the sage might attain equality with the God, the organization of the Epicurean group remained steadfastly hierarchical.[19] It would not be inappropriate to conclude, then, that the Epicurean conception of imitation of God is not so different from those of Pythagoras and Plato, except in those rare and extraordinary moments when a sage might attain perfection.[20] Furthermore, the philosopher is still the mediating figure in the mimetic relationship of the non-philosopher to God.

The Stoic tradition does not offer a unified position on the notion of imitation of God. The term mimesis is found only once in Arnim's collection of ancient Stoic fragments (Arnim 1986: 3:233) and there the context is a comparison of poetry and music, which are both characterized as mimetic arts. The language of *homoiôsis theô*, which one finds in Plato and other philosophical contexts, is also uncommon in Stoic discourse. Merki states categorically that the notion played no role whatsoever in earliest Stoicism (Merki 1952:7), and only later did the idea begin to have a place in Stoic thought.[21]

Merki is certainly correct that the notion did not play a central role in Stoic thought, and in some sense could not, given the theological assumptions of Stoicism, namely, that God is everywhere and everything is divine. Nevertheless, one can find examples which seem to parallel those already cited in this discussion. Epictetus, for example, in one of the few passages where the *homoiôsis theô* language appears, describes the relationship between the human and the divine as a mimetic relationship:

> The man who is going to please and obey them [the gods] must endeavor as best he can to resemble (*exomoiousthai*) them. If the deity is faithful, he must also be faithful; . . . if highminded, he also must be highminded, and so forth; therefore, in everything he says and does, he must act as an imitator (*zêlôtên*) of God. (Epict., *Diss.* 2.14.13)

Elsewhere, Epictetus characterizes the true Stoic as "a man who has set his heart upon changing from a man into a god" (Epict., *Diss.* 3.19.27). Likewise, Seneca argues that there is a fundamental link between the human and the divine, based on the intimacy of imitation:

> Rather there is a tie of relationship and a likeness (*similitudo*) [between God and humans], since in truth, a good man differs from God in the element of time only; he is God's pupil, his imitator (*æmulator*), and true offspring. (Sen., *Mor.* 1.5)

In another text (*De Ira* 2.16), Seneca argues that the ability to imitate is characteristically and uniquely human. Cicero, for his part, states that the path to God exists for those souls of the dead which "in the bodies of men had followed (*imitati*) the life of the gods" (Cic., *Tusc.* 1.72; see also *Leg. Man.* 1.25-26).

On this subject, the Cynic epistles are not dissimilar to the other sources in Greco-Roman antiquity (Malherbe). In Heraclitus' fifth letter, for example, there is this statement:

> Health is primary, and nature has the greatest skill in healing. The original, unskilled way of healing does not imitate what is contrary to nature, but later men imitated things of a different sort, and called their ignorance knowledge. But as for men, since I understand the nature of the world, I understand also that of man, I understand diseases, I understand health. I shall imitate God who, by commanding the sun, brings the excesses of the world into balance.[22]

In contrast to the Graeco-Roman tradition, in which the relationship between humanity and divinity is commonly described as mimetic, both the language of mimesis and the idea of the imitation of God are completely absent from the canonical Septuagint, and appear only sporadically in Hellenistic Jewish writings (Abrahams 1924; Buber 1926; Gulin 1925; Koch 1964; Marmorstein 1950). One of the few examples can be found in the *Testament of Asher* 4:3: "[The good individual] imitates the Lord, not accepting the seeming good as though it were the truly good" (Charlesworth 1:817). In addition, one can find a handful of similar statements in the *Letter of Aristeas*, here in the context of advising a king concerning his just reign.[23]

The notion of imitating God also appears in the work of Philo, who not only invokes the notion, but actually quotes the fundamental Platonic text on *homoiôsis theô* (*Tht.* 176B) at one point (Philo, *Fug.* 63). In *On the Virtues*, Philo says, " . . . a man should imitate God (*mimeisthai theon*) as much as may be and leave nothing undone that may promote such assimilation as is possible" (*Virt.* 168). Elsewhere he writes, " . . . to imitate God's works is a pious act" (*Leg. All.* 1.48), and asks, "what greater good can there be than that they [humans] should imitate God?" (*Spec. Leg.* 4.73) One striking motif in Philo's invocation of the notion of imitation of God is his analogy between the parental relationship to children and God's relationship to the world. For example, in his work *On the Decalogue*, he writes:

> For parents are the servants of God for the task of begetting children, and he who dishonors the servant dishonors also the Lord. Some bolder spirits, glorifying the name of parenthood, say that a father and a mother are in fact gods revealed to sight who copy (*mimoumenoi*) the Uncreated in his work as the Framer of life. He, they say, is the God or Maker of the world, they of those only whom they have begotten, and how can reverence be rendered to the invisible God by those who show irreverence to the gods who are near at hand and seen by the eye? (*Decal.* 119-120)[24]

These examples from Philo and other Hellenistic Jewish texts are, however, important exceptions in ancient Jewish literature. The idea of imitating God was not a prevailing Jewish notion. No term parallel to imitation of God, assimilation to God, or following God appears in the Hebrew Bible. Where such notions do occur, it is only in Jewish literature produced during the Hellenistic period, and most predominantly in the work of Philo, upon whom the influence of Platonic thought is well-known.

IMITATION IN KINGSHIP

Related to the general notion of imitation of God is the idea that the king is the privileged emulator of God. One can easily see how this idea would develop within the Platonic sphere, where the philosopher was described as the special imitator of God and where the philosopher-king was considered the best of human possibilities. But the king as a special case in the realm of divine imitation is a broader and more general idea within Hellenistic political philosophy as a whole.[25]

An early example of this special kind of imitation may be found in Isocrates's oration *To Philip*, where Isocrates invokes the model of Heracles as both ancestor and god:

> Now, while all who are blessed with understanding ought to set before themselves the greatest of men as their model, and strive to become like him, it behoves you above all to do so. For since you have no need to follow alien examples but have before you one from your own house, have we not then the right to expect that you will be spurred on by this and inspired by the ambition to make yourself like the ancestor of your race? I do not mean that you will be able to imitate Heracles in all his exploits; for even among the gods there are some who could not do that; but in the qualities of the spirit, in devotion to humanity, and in the good will which he cherished toward the Hellenes, you can come close to his purposes. (Isoc., *Ep. ad Phil.* 113-114)[26]

Aristotle also articulates the notion that the imitation of God is the special purview of the king. In his terms, the responsibility of government belongs to the one who, on account of leading a superior life and possessing remarkable achievements, would resemble a god (Arist., *Pol.* 1259B, 1326A).

The king as the privileged imitator of God appears as a fundamental theme in the fragments preserved in Stobaeus's chapter, *Peri Basileias* (*On Kingship*). In this collection of discourse on the appropriate execution of royal power, two important aspects of imitation are stressed. The first lies in the analogies drawn between god and the king, the universe and the state, objects in the world and subjects in the king's realm. The second is the emphasis on harmony in the state as a copy of cosmic order. These two aspects are succinctly expressed in a passage from Diotogenes, quoted in Stobaeus:

> The king bears the same relation to the state as God to the world; and the state is in the same ratio to the world as the king is to God. For the state, made as it is by the harmonizing of many different elements, is an imitation of the order and harmony of the world, while the king who has an absolute rulership, and is himself animate law, has been transformed into a deity among men. (Stob., *Ecl.* 4.7.61; Goodenough 1928:65; Dvornik 1966:249)

Dvornik attributes this combination of notions to a Pythagorean origin, and certainly the invocation of the idea of harmony here echoes the Pythagorean cosmology described above (Dvornik 1966:249 citing Delatte 1942). In any case, what is striking about this combination of ideas—the imitation of God by the king and the analogy between harmony among the king's subjects and cosmic order—is that imitation and harmony are explicitly bound together within a particular discourse about political power. The notion of harmony here has to do with things being in their proper places and performing their proper functions. Political discord becomes analogous to cosmic discord. The notion of the king as the privileged imitator of God emerges specifically in hellenistic political philosophy, the social function of which is to rationalize an emergent absolute monarchy ruled by a divinized king. One can see easily here how the discourse of kingship operates to undergird a system of power, so that the analogies between God/king, cosmos/state, created beings/royal subjects function to shore up the innate quality of the king's power[27] and to heighten the crime of political discord by describing it in cosmic terms.

The king also functions as a model for his subjects, who will imitate him just as he imitates God. The second fragment attributed to Ecphantus in Stobaeus demonstrates this point:

> Rather, it seems to me, by offering Himself as one worthy of imitation God implants a desire to imitate Him in every man who has a nature like God's. God is Himself good, and to be so is His sole and easy function, while those who imitate Him do as a consequence all things better than other people. The resemblance which each man can achieve consists in self-sufficiency. . . . Now the earthly king would be just as self-sufficient as the rest of us (by imitating God). For in making himself like God he would make himself like the Most Powerful. . . . Now when matters are put upon subjects by force and necessity their individual zeal for imitation is impossible, and nothing diminishes good will like fear . . . . The king is capable of putting this good into human nature so that by imitation of him, their Better, they will follow in the way they should go.[28]

For all the valorization of the mimetic relationship in this kingship discourse, the mimetic is still considered to be a derivative relationship. The distance between the model and the copy is never completely erased; the copy is related to the model by means of analogy, and it is from that analogy that the copy gains its power. Nevertheless, it remains that the copy is a derivation from the perfection of the model:

> The king must be a wise man, for so he will be a copy and imitator of the first God. For God is the first king and ruler by nature, while the other is so only by birth and imitation. The one rules in the entire universe, the other upon earth; and the one lives and rules all things forever and possesses wisdom (*sophia*) in himself, the other is temporal and has only understanding (*epistêmê*). (Sthenidas of Locri, in Stob., *Ecl.* 4.7.63; Dvornik 1966:252-253)[29]

One last aspect of this literature on kingship which bears comment is the imagery of fatherhood which is invoked within it. Diotogenes calls upon kings to imitate the majesty of Zeus, and highlights the role of Zeus as the father of gods and men (Dvornik 1966:250; Diotogenes in Stob., *Ecl.* 4.7.61; Good-enough 1928:65-66). Pseudo-Sthenidas of Locri ties the imita-tion of God by the king to the king's role as the father of his subjects (Stob., *Ecl.* 4.7.63; Dvornik 1966:252); and to Ecphan-tus is attributed this statement:

> . . . there must exist complete good will, first, on the part of the king toward his subjects and, second, on the part of these toward the king, such as is felt by a father toward his son, by a shepherd toward his sheep, and by a law toward those who use it. (Stob., *Ecl.* 4.7.64-66; Dvornik 1966:255)

The imitation of Zeus and the concomitant image of the king as father of his subjects recurs in many writers in the Hellenistic and Roman periods,[30] and Dvornik emphasizes the importance of this imagery for early Christian political thought (Dvornik 1966:541). As we shall see, this imagery and the analogy between god/king/father are also significant for the analysis of the Pauline use of mimesis.

To summarize the importance of this particular aspect of imitation in ancient discourse, one should note two things in particular. First, the analogies God/king, cosmos/state, cre-ation/subjects create the possibility for a divine justification for political realities. Mimesis in this context serves a particularly conservative function by providing the matrix for sustaining power relationships. The second point is related to the first, and has to do with the mobilization of the notion of harmony as a value. The mimetic relationship replicates the harmonious quality of the cosmos; sameness and the desire to achieve it are tied to the cosmic order. By inference, difference is relegated to the realm of discord and chaos.

EDUCATIONAL AND ETHICAL MIMESIS

Werner Jaeger's classic study, *Paideia: The Ideals of Greek Culture*, charts the development of Greek education from the earliest periods, when it possessed an aristocratic and private character, to later times when the *polis* stood as the privileged social and political institution and when the educational system

was transformed to produce citizens whose values were conso-
nant with their new civic responsibilities. Jaeger characterizes
the transformation of the older aristocratic values to the new
civic values in this way:

> From Homer onwards, aristocratic education was governed by
> the idea of following noble examples. A great man is a physi-
> cal embodiment of the man which the pupil must follow, and
> the pupil's admiration for his ideal qualities naturally prompts
> him to imitate them. This personal factor in imitation (*mimêsis*)
> disappears when the laws provide the pattern. In the graduat-
> ed system of education described by Protagoras [Plato, *Prt.*
> 326C-D], it has not wholly disappeared, but has been relegat-
> ed to a lower place: it is now part of the elementary courses
> of instruction in poetry, which are devoted to explanation of
> the content alone, with emphasis on the moral maxims and
> historical examples which it embodies rather than on the form
> which develops rhythm and harmony in the spirit. (Jaeger
> 1945:1:310)

The Greek ideals of education were based originally on imitation, and then eventually were reduced to imitation of "stock"
notions and figures. Nevertheless, the notion of imitation remained central to pedagogical ideas throughout the classical
and Hellenistic periods and continued, with variations, into the
Roman period.[31]

The origins of the human capacity to learn were understood
to be imitative in nature. For example, Plutarch cites Democritus's understanding of the origins of culture, art, and technology
as imitations of the natural world:

> Democritus declares that we [humans] have been their [ani-
> mals'] pupils in matters of fundamental importance: of the
> spider in weaving and mending, of the swallow in homebuild-
> ing, of the sweet-voiced swan and nightingale in our imitation
> of their song. (Plu., *De soll. an.* 20 [*Mor.* 974A])

Aristotle states in his *Poetics* that humans learn first by imitation:

> Imitation is natural to man from childhood, one of his advan-
> tages over the lower animals being this, that he is the most
> imitative creature in the world, and learns at first by imitation.

And it is also natural for all to delight in works of imitation. (Arist., *Poet.* 1448B)

The idea of a mimetic teacher-disciple relationship pervades the ancient Greek understanding of education. Xenophon, in his defense of Socrates in the first book of his *Memorabilia*, describes this relationship between the philosopher-teacher and his students:

> To be sure he never professed to teach this [the desire for goodness]: but by letting his own light shine, he led his disciples to hope that they through imitation of him would attain such excellence. (Xen., *Mem.* 1.2.3)[32]

Isocrates, the rhetorician and teacher, was particularly concerned with the role of imitation in his teaching. In his treatise, *Against the Sophists*, Isocrates writes of the importance of the mimetic function in the classroom:

> . . . [A]nd the teacher, for his part, must so expound the principles of the art with the utmost possible exactness as to leave out nothing that can be taught, and, for the rest, he must in himself set such an example (*paradeigma*) of oratory that the students who have taken form (*ektupôthentas*) under his instruction and are able to pattern (*mimêsasthai*) after him will, from the outset, show in their speaking a degree of grace and charm which is not found in others. (Isoc., *Soph.* 17; see Jaeger 1945:3:64)

Isocrates's emphasis on the importance of the teacher's example in the rhetorical education of pupils is but one expression of the commonplace role of imitation in rhetorical training from the classical period right through to the Roman period.[33] While the notion of imitation was widespread in antiquity, within the context of rhetorical education mimesis had a fairly limited set of associations (Kennedy 1980:116-119). The teaching methods of the sophists were based on imitation. Later, during the Hellenistic period, grammarians began to devise canons of models within the specific literary genres. Homer was a model for epic while the Ten Attic Orators became the models for oratory. The earliest work dedicated specifically to rhetorical imitation is Dionysius of Halicarnassus's *On Imitation*, which was composed toward the end of the first century BCE and which is preserved only in fragments.[34] Later works, specifically Book 10 of Quintilian's *Institutio Oratoria* (Quint., *Inst.* 10.2), the treatise *On the Sublime* spuriously attributed to Longinus ([Longinus], *Subl.* 13), and Hermogenes's *On Ideas of Style* (Hermog., *Id.* 1), continued to emphasize the importance of imitation in rhetorical education and practice.

In the realm of Roman literature, imitation of "the purest and simplest" Greek models became the primary goal of the Atticist movement. This movement was not wholly uncontroversial, as Cicero's attempts to counteract it aptly attest. Nevertheless, Atticism, with its focus on imitation of older Greek models, remained a strong influence over rhetorical practice through the second century CE within the second sophistic and throughout the Byzantine period (Kennedy 1980:118-119).

The interconnectedness of this rather narrow understanding of imitation—imitation of ancient models in rhetorical education and practice—with a broader understanding of imitation as an ethical value may be seen in the role of imitation in what Kennedy calls "Augustan rhetoric" (Kennedy 1972:383). Here he points out a parallel between, on the one hand, the imitation of literary models from the past in order to achieve excellence in rhetoric and, on the other, the moral imitation of virtuous models from the past with the goal of achieving an exemplary mode of life.[35] He continues with a description of the rhetorical character of the Forum which was constructed during Augustus's reign. Architecturally, the Forum forces the leaders and the citizens to be literally surrounded by exemplars from the past (Kennedy 1972:383; MacKendrick 1960:145-150).

Generally speaking, educational imitation and ethical imitation are often collapsed into a single notion in ancient discourse. This is logical, given the role of the educational system to inculcate certain values and virtues in its students. In Plato, for example, one finds the two conflated in his explanation of the importance of reading the good poets:

> The masters take pains accordingly, and the children, when they have learnt their letters and are getting to understand the written word as before they did only the spoken, are furnished

with works of good poets to read as they sit in class, and are made to learn them off by heart: here they meet with many admonitions, many descriptions and praises and eulogies of good men in times past, that the boy in envy (*zêlôn*) may imitate them and yearn to become even as they. (Pl., *Prt.* 325E-326A)

Likewise, one finds maxim-like advice in the writings of Isocrates, in which the ethical and the educational are intertwined:

Pattern after the character of kings, and follow closely their ways. (Isoc., *Ep. ad Dem.* 36)

If there are men whose reputations you envy (*zêlois*), imitate their deeds. (Isoc., *Ep. ad Nic.* 38)

Be not satisfied with praising good men, but imitate them as well. (Isoc., *Ep. ad Nic.* 61)

Ethical notions of imitation have a strong and ancient lineage. Some of the most ancient philosophical fragments contain references to ethical imitation of good,[36] and ethical imitation of older models is commonplace in the Platonic and Aristotelian traditions, as well as in Stoic and Cynic texts. Strikingly, it is within the category of ethical imitation that one finds the strongest Hellenistic Jewish emphasis. Philo calls for the imitation of particular virtuous figures, most notably Moses,[37] and Josephus's *Jewish Antiquities* makes numerous references to ethical imitation of both the positive and negative exemplars, often to particular figures from the past.[38]

It is clear from even these few examples that the imitation of a teacher or a model in the educational systems of Greco-Roman antiquity and in the ethical positions of both pagan and Jewish writers is a fundamental category. The disciple is understood to be an impressionable person to be molded (hence the language of "modelling," "stamping," "shaping") (Jaeger 1945:3:64), and the role of the teacher/model is one of authoritative example (see Marrou 1982:Part I). In addition, the educational system as a whole is patterned on the notion that sameness is tied to adaptation and harmony, that the pupil who imitates well will function best in the society for which he is being trained.

THE SIGNIFICANCE OF MIMESIS IN THE DISCOURSES
OF GRECO-ROMAN ANTIQUITY

Such a sweeping survey of uses of mimesis will not produce a monolithic definition that can form the backdrop to an examination of Paul's use of the term. Nevertheless, several common features recur in the variety of discourses examined in this chapter. These features are not always explicit, but are often presupposed in the ways that the term mimesis is employed.

The features are interrelated and reinscribe each other. First of all, mimesis is constituted through a hierarchy in which the model is imbued with perfection and wholeness, and the copy represents an attempt to reclaim that perfection. This relationship is perhaps most clearly seen in the cosmological discourse of Plato's *Timaeus*. Here cosmic hierarchies are constructed in mimetic fashion and each descending level of being is a dimmer reflection of the level above it. Because of this hierarchical nature of mimetic relation, mimesis becomes a derivative function, in that it attempts to reproduce an unattainable origin.

Furthermore, because of the superior value which is bestowed upon the model in the mimetic system, the question of authority is foregrounded in the mimetic relationship; the model has authority to which the copy submits.

Finally, sameness is valued above difference, and this valuing undergirds the entire mimetic relationship. This elevation of sameness creates a tension in the mimetic relationship, which incorporates both a drive toward sameness and a need for hierarchy. The copy aims at sameness, but can never attain that sameness because of the hierarchical nature of its relation to the model. Moreover, linked with sameness are a series of other values: unity, harmony, and order. Sameness and unity and harmony have positive value while, by implication, difference is associated with disunity and discord. This treatment of difference has profound implications for processes of social formation, because it suggests that difference must be subversive of unity, harmony, and order.[39]

In the chapter that follows, I will work out the implications of these observations about imitation in antiquity for Paul's own discourse of mimesis. The identification of imitation with the drive toward unity and nondifference is apparent in Paul's writings. However, he has also incorporated the other values associated with mimesis which have been identified in this chapter. Further, as we shall see, the language of imitation, with its concomitant tension between the drive toward sameness and the inherent hierarchy of the mimetic relationship, masks the will to power which one finds in Pauline discourse. Paul's appropriation of the discourse of mimesis is a powerful rhetorical move, because this language identifies the fundamental values of wholeness and unity with Paul's own privileged position vis-à-vis the gospel, the early Christian communities he founded and supervises, and Christ himself. Here is precisely where he makes his coercive move. To stand for anything other than what the apostle stands for is to articulate for oneself a place of difference, which has already implicitly been associated with discord and disorder. To stand in a position of difference is to stand in opposition, therefore, to the gospel, the community, and Christ.

4

"BE IMITATORS OF ME": DISCOURSES OF MIMESIS IN PAUL

Having established our theoretical and philological contours, we are now in a position to read the texts in which Paul uses the language of mimesis. Following the conclusions reached so far, our readings presuppose that Paul's discourse of mimesis is not a simply or naïvely pragmatic discourse, as some would hold. On the contrary, his use of the mimesis word group, completely naturalized in the Greek of his time, evokes for a first-century audience the whole range of associations outlined in the last chapter. Mimesis must be understood in its larger context, as a notion that places sameness at a premium and imbues the model with a privileged and unattainable status. From a Foucauldian perspective, Paul's rhetoric of mimesis prompts many questions about the political nature of the relationships between authorship and authority (including who speaks and who is silent), and the ways in which discourse and its control reinscribe and rationalize power relations. All of these associations set Paul's use of mimesis in a complex structural and thematic web that resists reduction to a simple explanation of social expediency.

The word (sum)*mimêtês* ("mimesis") appears in three of Paul's letters: 1 Thessalonians, Philippians, and 1 Corinthians. Some commentators have included with these passages Galatians 4:12 ("become as I am") as another mimetic exhortation, though no word related to *mimêtês* appears in the command (Schütz 1975:250-251; de Boer 1962:188-196). This study will limit itself to detailed readings of the passages in which the word *mimêtês* appears, though it will also include a brief examination of the Galatians passage. The argument put forward about the texts in which *mimêtês* actually occurs will be found to be sustainable in the case of the Galatians text as well.

1 THESSALONIANS 1:6-7, 2:14

1 Thessalonians 1:6

Paul's first reference to mimesis appears in the first thanksgiving section of 1 Thessalonians, where Paul praises the faithfulness of this community of Christians:

> We give thanks to God always for you all, constantly mentioning you in our prayers, remembering before our God and Father your work of faith and labor of love and steadfastness of hope in our Lord Jesus Christ. For we know, brethren beloved by God, that he has chosen you; for our gospel came to you not only in word, but also in power and in the Holy Spirit and with full conviction. You know what kind of men we proved to be among you for your sake (*kathôs oidate hoioi egenêthêmen [en] humin di' humas*). And you became imitators of us and of the Lord (*kai humeis mimêtai hêmôn egenêthête kai tou kuriou*), for you received the word in much affliction, with joy inspired by the Holy Spirit; so that you became an example to all the believers in Macedonia and in Achaia. (1 Thess 1:2-7)

At first, this text appears fairly straightforward; the Thessalonians have become *mimêtai* ("imitators") through their reception of the word, in spite of suffering. However, the syntactical construction of verse 6 suggests more nuances. Paul writes, literally: "and imitators of us you became, and of the Lord."

The word order in Greek (*egenēthēte* between *hēmōn* and *kai tou kuriou*) suggests that "and of the Lord" is a self-correction (Dobschütz 1909:72; Dibelius 1937:5; Neil 1950:18) or an afterthought (Stanley 1959:866). Some scholars have attempted to explain this uncomfortable construction by suggesting that the order—first Paul, and then the Lord—expresses the historical order in which the Thessalonians would have practiced their imitation, the Lord's example preceding Paul's historically (Neil 1950:18; Morris 1959:58). Rigaux's commentary (1950: 381) tries to smooth out the difficulty by connecting this text with Paul's exhortation in 1 Cor 11:1, where imitation of Paul is linked to Paul's imitation of Christ. Betz (1967:143-44) reaches a similar conclusion, arguing that it is through the reception of the gospel and its subsequent preaching that the Thessalonians have become imitators of Paul and the Lord. De Boer follows one of Michaelis's suggestions: the construction is not self-correction but rather a way of expanding upon the praise and recognition which the community's behavior has earned.[1]

In their attempt to obviate the self-correcting aspect of the construction, these readings risk overlooking the confusion of identity which Paul's sentence expresses. Indeed from the perspective of the letter's larger context, such confusion appears from the very start. In the salutation at the beginning, the letter's authorship is attributed to Paul, Silvanus, and Timothy, and the first-person plural voice dominates the letter's discourse.[2] This is not a particularly problematic point, except at certain revealing junctures in the text. For example, most relevantly at 1:5, Paul writes, "for our gospel (*to euangelion hēmōn*) came to you not only in word, but also in power and in the Holy Spirit and with full conviction." Does he mean the gospel of Silvanus, Timothy, and Paul? Or their gospel and that of the Lord?

Stanley attempts to explain this difficulty by claiming that "the Pauline notion of the Gospel is rather that it is a divine-human Word, containing not only God's self-revelation but also an element personal to the preacher, viz. his faith's testimony to the truth of what he proclaims" (Stanley 1959:864 n. 1). Such an explanation might well be right, but it is nevertheless insufficient, because Paul is not arguing that *any* preacher's gospel is a viable appropriation of revelation. He is insisting that *his* rendering of that revelation is acceptable. Therefore, his appropriation of the gospel as "our gospel" is implicitly a statement about who speaks with authority and who does not. Later in the letter when Paul refers to the gospel, he calls it "the gospel of God" (*to euangelion tou theou*, 2:2, 8, 9) or "the gospel of Christ" (*to euangelion tou Christou*, 3:2). That is, "our gospel" in 1:5 is equivalent to "the gospel of God" and "the gospel of Christ." The equivalence which is set up, then, can be read as a rhetorical attempt to undergird the authority of Paul's message by equating it with God and Christ.[3]

The usage of *mimētēs* in both passages in 1 Thessalonians differs from the other passages (Phil 3:17 and 1 Cor 4:16, 11:1) because the Thessalonians texts describe a historical "fact" about mimesis, rather than exhorting the community to perform a mimetic act. This distinction proves especially important for Betz (1967:143) and Schütz (1975:226). In syntactical terms, the difference lies in the use here of the indicative, whereas Paul uses the imperative in the other texts.[4] The import of this distinction is twofold. First and more obviously, Paul uses the indicative here (and at 2:14) to describe a particular reality, to characterize the behavior of the Thessalonian community. It is not an exhortation, but a clear statement of what is actually the case. Second, the syntactical distinction operates at the level of rhetoric, to place the Thessalonian community in a special position vis-à-vis other communities, and to heighten the praise which Paul is offering the community. The Thessalonians have performed their mimetic role (as imitators of Paul and the Lord) so that they have obtained an additional function in the mimetic economy: they have themselves become the model (*tupos*) for the Macedonian and Achaian communities. They have moved in this somewhat fluid system to perform a mediating role, as models for imitation by others.

But, of what exactly does such praiseworthy imitation consist? In verse 6, the participle *dexamenoi* ("having received") modifies the main verb, *egenēthēte* ("you became").

The imitation of Paul and of the Lord therefore must be somehow located in this act of receiving the word. Further, the participle itself is modified by the prepositional phrases, "in much affliction" and "with the joy of the Holy Spirit." In addition, because the Thessalonians' imitation became an example for the communities in Macedonia and Achaia, the character of the imitation must have to do with the *manner* in which the Thessalonians imitated Paul and the Lord. That is to say, since those other communities have already presumably "received the word," the example which the Thessalonians offer lies in the way in which they have received it.

The nature of the affliction (*thlipsis*) which characterizes the community's reception of the word is unclear. What *is* clear is that it is an affliction which connects the community to Paul and to the Lord—and later, at 2:14, to the communities in Judea—affliction that has to do with suffering persecution at the hands of surrounding communities.

1 Thessalonians 2:14

1 Thess 2:14 occurs in the letter's second thanksgiving section. Here the imitation in question is not that of Paul or of the Lord, but of the churches in Judea which have suffered persecution:

> And we also thank God constantly for this, that when you received the word of God which you heard from us, you accepted it not as the word of men but as what it really is, the word of God which is at work in you believers. For you, brethren, became imitators (*humeis gar mimêtai egenêthête*) of the churches of God in Christ Jesus which are in Judea; for you suffered the same things from your own countrymen (*hoti ta auta epathete kai humeis hupo tôn idiôn sumphuletôn*) as they did from the Jews, who killed both the Lord Jesus and the prophets, and drove us out, and displease God and oppose all men by hindering us from speaking to the Gentiles that they may be saved—so as always to fill up the measure of their sins. But God's wrath has come upon them at last! (1 Thess 2:13-16)

This passage has provoked debate about its authenticity, motivated in part by its explicit anti-Semitism.[5] The arguments

against its authenticity have been made primarily on comparative grounds—that is, that Paul's view of Judaism can be shown
to be more positive in other texts. While this may be the case,
Hurd's observation that it is methodologically dangerous to
attempt to harmonize the various Pauline epistles when the
letter itself must be considered the exegetical unit, must be
taken seriously. Regardless of the final judgment on this question, the rhetorical effect within the letter itself remains, and it
is to this effect that our attention now turns.

There is a notably passive quality to the imitation described
in this passage (Stanley 1959:865, 867; Michaelis 1967:670;
Schütz 1975:227-228; Masson 1957:21). The verb in the phrase
mimêtai egenêthête ("you became imitators") is a passive form
and is sometimes taken to imply God as agent (Masson 1957:
21). The verb *epathete* ("you suffered"), though not a passive
form, conveys a clear passive sense here in its conjunction with
the preposition *hupo* ("you suffered under/at the hands of"; cf.
NEB, "you have been treated by"). Even the activity for which
the Thessalonians are initially praised has a passive quality,
namely their acceptance (*dexesthai*) of the word of God from
Paul as they received (*paralambanein*) it.

For Paul, this passivity is laudable; the Thessalonians are to
be praised for their receptivity to Paul's gospel, as is clear in
this passage and in chapter 1. They have been inserted into the
mimetic economy and performed their receptive function well;
they have endured suffering in imitation of Paul, the Lord, and
the Judean churches. Their act of mimesis is distinct from the
exhortations elsewhere for other communities to become Paul's
imitators. Here, they have achieved their mimetic goal in an
existential way, and have themselves become models for others.[6] Their suffering, for which they are praised by Paul in both
the passages, ties their experience to that of everyone else in
the mimetic system: Paul, the Lord, and the other persecuted
communities. In becoming imitators of others' sufferings, their
experience is structurally linked to that of all these other persecuted ones. Their sufferings become a way of establishing
identity within the group and in the face of "outsiders," a way
for Paul both to praise them and to claim them.

The mimetic relationship articulated here does not reveal the clearly defined relations of power evident in the other texts involving mimesis. Nevertheless, there are reasons for including these texts under this general interpretation, among them the confusion of identity which is evident in the statement "you became imitators of me and of the Lord" and in the characterization of the gospel sometimes as "our gospel" and other times as "Christ's gospel" or "God's gospel." Also, the passive nature of the imitation described in 1 Thessalonians 2 points to the power relations involved in such imitation. One might ask what implications this kind of passivity might have for how the early Christian community was to be constituted, and how "the word" was to be appropriated.

PHILIPPIANS 3:17

When Paul writes to the community in Philippi, he exhorts his readers to become his imitators as part of a larger call to unity within the community (Stanley 1959:870-871). The passage reads:

> Let those of us who are mature be thus minded; and if in anything you are otherwise minded, God will reveal that also to you. Only let us hold true to what we have attained. Brethren, join in imitating me (summimêtai mou ginesthe), and mark those who so live as you have an example in us. For many, of whom I have often told you and now tell you even with tears, live as enemies of the cross of Christ. Their end is destruction, their god is the belly, and they glory in their shame, with minds set on earthly things. But our commonwealth is in heaven, and from it we await a Savior, the Lord Jesus Christ, who will change our lowly body to be like his glorious body, by the power which enables him even to subject all things to himself. (Phil 3:15-21)

Several observations can be made about the effect of this rhetoric. First of all, Paul articulates a clear contrast between the "brethren" who are exhorted to join in imitating him, and those who live as enemies of the cross of Christ. His use of the peculiar form, sum-mimêtês, reinforces the notion of creating unity in this action.[7] The implication is that those who do not join in imitating Paul are enemies of the cross of Christ. The contrast between the fates of the two groups is drawn in striking imagery.

Second, the passage constructs a clearly drawn hierarchy at whose head is Jesus Christ who has the power to subject all things to himself. The imitation of Paul will allow the Philippian community access to the heavenly realm, which is governed by Christ; the hierarchy, Christ-Paul-Christians, is invoked as a justification for the call to unity under Paul's aegis. That is, the hierarchy functions in a double sense. First, it constructs the power relations that will give the community its identity as a monolithic social formation constituted by the unity it must maintain. Second, it reinscribes Paul's privileged position within the hierarchy as the mediating figure through whom the community might gain access to salvation.

The third important observation concerning this passage is its connection with the Christ hymn in chapter 2, in which the call to unity is also expressed.[8] The two passages are linked by a linguistic repetition: *touto phronômen* ("let us be of this mind") in 3:15 echoes *touto phroneite* ("[you] be of this mind") in 2:5 (Stanley 871). In chapter 2, the call to unity in the community is tied to the humility displayed by Jesus Christ in the crucifixion. The connections Paul draws here are striking. First, in chapter 2, he ties together, within his call to unity, the humility he wishes the community would demonstrate and the humility of the crucified Christ. Then, in 3:17, he connects his call for unity to his exhortation to the Philippians to join together as imitators of himself.

The impact of this rhetoric is powerful. Christian identity is linked, on the one hand, with the humility displayed by Christ on the cross and, on the other hand, with the imitation of Paul. There exists only one alternative to this identity, and that is to "live as enemies of the cross of Christ" for whom "their end is destruction, their god is the belly, and they glory in their shame, with minds set on earthly things." These two identities—the Christian and the non-Christian—are set up as polar opposites; practicing humility like that of the crucified Christ and imitating Paul promise a heavenly transformation while the rejection of these paths assures destruction. Therefore, the unity that is demanded in Paul's discourse, unity that grows out of both the imitation of Paul and the practice of humility akin to that exhibited by the crucified Christ, means a commonality against the polar opposite, those who face certain destruction. The lines between the "insiders" and the "outsiders" have been constructed ineluctably.

1 CORINTHIANS 4:16, 11:1

1 Corinthians offers the richest context for producing a reading of the discourse of mimesis in Paul's letters. First, 1 Corinthians is, in the language of literary criticism, a strong text: it is structurally coherent and self-conscious enough to sustain interrogation and interpretation. Second, on a thematic level, the letter is concerned with a collection of issues that mirror the theoretical concerns raised in chapter three above. The letter takes up questions of leadership and authority, order within the social body of the community, and the creation of harmony and unity among split factions. It is concerned with a fundamental determinant of social formation—who is inside and who is outside the boundaries of the social group and social identity. And it is fundamentally interested in the discipline of individual bodies within the social body.

These aspects of social formation have been routinely linked conceptually in 1 Corinthian scholarship, albeit often without explicit acknowledgment of the hermeneutical consequences of such a connection. De Boer, for example, writes in setting up the context for his interpretation of 1 Cor 4:16, "The strife and party spirit in which they [the Corinthians] lived gave ample evidence of how little their lives had been captivated by true spirituality. Rather, a basic carnality was incapacitating them from discerning spiritual things" (1962:139-140). While a rhetorical analysis of de Boer's interpretation is beyond the scope of this project, this sentence provides a dramatic, but not unique, example of how certain theological ideas and social arrangements are, in interpretation, considered to be self-evident. In this sentence, one sees de Boer as interpreter setting between himself and Paul no ironic distance whatsoever; Paul is the speaker-who-is-supposed-to-know, and his voice is cast as objective. Therefore, Paul's construction of the situation in Corinth takes on the contours of truth, and his linking of the concept of discord (absence of unity, difference) with the idea of undisciplined bodies (individual and social) is, for de Boer, self-evident.

It is my contention, however, that Paul's use of the notion of mimesis twice in this document, a document preoccupied with questions of social order and authority, is not completely fortuitous. The idea of mimesis—with all of its shades and nuances of meaning—is felicitously linked in Paul's discourse to notions of social order and power, and each reinscribes and reinforces the other's "truth." That Paul would exhort the Corinthians twice in this one document to become his imitators, when he is dealing with problems of social diffusion and dispersed authority, is both striking and telling.

1 Corinthians 4:16

Paul first invokes mimesis in 1 Corinthians at 4:16, at the end of his discussion of the appropriate relationship between the community and its leadership. The problems Paul is addressing have to do with various members of the community aligning themselves with one or another teacher or leader. Throughout the rhetoric of chapters 1 through 4 are imbedded calls to unity and sameness. Implicit in this rhetoric is the writer's claim upon the actions of the readers; to join with Paul as a spiritual person is to avoid the pitfalls to which everyone else is subject. But because Paul claims to be empty of all content but that of the gospel, to dispute with Paul is to dispute with the truth. Thus, the economies of unity and sameness are recast as truth.

At 1:10-18, one can see how this economy works. Paul first of all calls upon the Corinthians to resolve their disputes: "I appeal to you, brethren, by the name of our Lord Jesus Christ, that all of you agree and that there be no dissensions among you, but that you be united in the same mind and the same judgment" (1:10). Unity of mind is the clearest priority here; difference is imbued only with negative connotations, and it must be erased in order to reestablish order. 1:11-16 articulates the nature of the particular dispute over who has baptized and who, therefore, has authority. 1:17 describes Paul's self-ascribed role as mediation for the gospel. The emphasis here is on Paul's "contentless" nature; he is simply a conduit through which the gospel passes: "For Christ did not send me to baptize but to preach the gospel, and not with eloquent wisdom, lest the cross of Christ be emptied of its power." This is a clever rhetorical gesture, because it paradoxically ascribes to Paul both a privileged status vis-à-vis the gospel, bestowing upon Paul a special authority to speak, and also a contentlessness, an emptiness which removes him from the fray. He is the one who is supposed to speak while it is not he who speaks at all, but Christ through him. This gesture is followed by an uncompromising statement of the implications of the unity which has already been invoked: "For the word of the cross is folly to those who are perishing, but to us who are being saved it is the power of God" (1:18). Unity within the community constructs the community as "us who are being saved;" unity and sameness produce salvation, while difference ("those who are perishing," i.e., those who are not being saved, those who are different from "us") is damned to folly.

The argument here will be best served by moving forward to the passage which invokes mimesis (4:16). After making some preliminary observations about this passage, I will return to the text encircled rhetorically by these two summons to sameness—the call for unity in 1:10-17 and the call for imitation at 4:14-21.[9] I will argue that the three sections in between these two summons function as mimetic examples and building to a crescendo with the rhetorical force of 4:14-21.

The passage invoking mimesis occurs at the end of the discourse about unity, factionalism and correct knowledge:

> I do not write this to make you ashamed, but to admonish you as my beloved children. For though you have countless guides (*paidagôgous*) in Christ, you do not have many fathers. For I became your father in Christ Jesus through the Gospel. I urge you, then, be imitators of me (*Parakalô oun humas, mimêtai mou ginesthe*). Therefore I sent to you Timothy, my beloved and faithful child in the Lord, to remind you of my ways in

Christ, as I teach them everywhere in every church (1 Cor 4:14-17).

The patriarchal image is striking in this passage; Paul understands himself as a father to the Corinthian community and to Timothy, his emissary.[10] Commentators have almost all understood this paternal metaphor to evoke a sense of kindness and love. Conzelmann, for example, describes the shift in tone at verse 14 as Paul speaking in a "conciliatory fashion" (Conzelmann 1975:91), while Sanders describes Paul's tone as one of "paternal concern tempered by his deeper affection" (Sanders 1959:353). De Boer states that, "His only intention was to do what every good father does; he was admonishing his children with love" (de Boer 1962:145). Benjamin Fiore goes to even greater lengths to argue for the appropriateness of this paternal love and concern, by citing a passage from Epictetus about the suitability of a father's overseeing the activities of the others in the family (Fiore 1982:325-326 n. 27). In his note, however, he quotes selectively from the passage. The passage follows:

> When he sees that he has watched over men, and toiled in their behalf; and that he has slept in purity, while his sleep leaves him even purer than he was before; and that every thought which he thinks is that of a friend and servant to the gods, of one who shares in the government of Zeus; . . . why should he not have courage to speak freely to his own brothers, to his children, in a word, to his kinsmen? That is why the man who is in this frame of mind is neither a busybody nor a meddler; for he is not meddling in other people's affairs when he is overseeing the actions of men, but these are his proper concern. (Epict., *Diss.* 3.22.95ff)

Fiore ends his citation at this point in the text, thereby demonstrating that it is within the proper domain of the father to oversee the activities of family members. But the passage continues, in a way which casts the role of the father in parallel imagery with another social role:

> Otherwise, go call the general a meddler when he oversees and reviews and watches over his troops, and punishes those who are guilty of a breach of discipline. (Epict.,*Diss.* 3.22.95ff)

The paternal imagery here is set in clear analogy with a military image. Whatever else one might want to claim about the relationship between a general and his troops, it is difficult to imagine that the general acts out of love and kind feeling. The appropriateness of the father's exercise of authority in the family is being paralleled here with the general's exertion of authority.

My point is that the image of the father must be read in cultural context, that is, in relationship to the nature of the paternal role in Greco-Roman society—which is a role of possessing total authority over children.[11] In addition, in the cosmological descriptions which make use of mimesis-language, the role of the parent is delineated as ontologically superior to that of the offspring, specifically because the creative role of the parent is viewed as analogous to the divine creative function, as the discussion in the previous chapter demonstrated. Furthermore, as one now knows from the many salient (especially feminist) critiques of the powerful symbolic function of the paternal image in religious texts from antiquity (see Ochshorn 1981; Trible 1978; Daly 1973; Schüssler Fiorenza 1984, esp. chapter 2), naïve and utopian readings of Paul's use of this image are no longer justifiable.

Not all scholars, however, have understood the father image in such benign terms. Donald Williams, for example, assumes that it evokes "the authoritarian position of father-teacher" (Williams 1967:165). Bengt Holmberg understands the father-child relationship articulated in Paul's letters to be one of obligation on the part of the child toward the father, although he characterizes the relation as affectionate (Holmberg 1980:77-79). Holmberg also ties the idea of Paul's fatherhood of the early communities directly to the call to imitation. He writes (1980:78): "The call to imitate the apostle is a consequence of the father-child relation and may be indirect evidence that this is considered to exist even where we only meet the exhortation to imitate Paul." Norman Petersen also vacillates between stating categorically the authoritative nature of the father-child relationship—something which he is willing to acknowledge in theory—and articulating for Paul a role which is somehow less offensive to modern sensibilities (Petersen 1985:130-131).[12] None of these scholars attempts to articulate any sort of reciprocity as part of the relationship between father and child.

There are other conclusions which might be drawn from the exhortation in 4:16 to become imitators of Paul. First of all, one might return to the observation that 4:16 is linked with 1:10 in its repetition of *parakalō humas*. Betz (1967:154-55) has offered the most thoroughgoing reading of the implications of this repetition. He argues decisively that the role of the apostle as a model in the mimetic relationship is a role of mediation. Furthermore, he sets that relationship explicitly in the realm of the community's obedience to the exhortation of Paul, who functions as mouthpiece for divine exhortation. Such a notion was encountered earlier, in the interpretation of 1:10-18, where it was argued that Paul's "contentlessness" could be interpreted as a rhetorical strategy that both constructs the apostle as the one speaking with authority and keeps his position sacrosanct because he is only the medium for the divine word.

Seen in its larger context of the discussion of the appropriate relationship between the Christian community and its leaders, 4:16 also has to do with unity. We have already seen the call to unity and sameness embodied in 1:10-18, with its implicit threat of the consequences of difference. The call to unity goes even further, however. Sanders has noted in his article on this text that Paul's theology of baptism in this section of 1 Corinthians differs from the baptismal theology found in Romans 6, precisely in the fact that in 1 Cor 1:13-17 Paul is invoking the unifying power of baptism for creating a collective, communal identity (Sanders 1981:360-362). The function of the baptismal rite for creating a group identity is double-edged, as is the call for unity: by creating group identity, it creates *de facto* an inside and an outside. The call for a resolution of divisiveness in this situation is strengthened by these two parallel exhortations in Paul's discourse: first, the call for unity which is shored up by the invocation of the power of baptism; second, the exhortation to become Paul's imitators. Both of these demand sameness. Both attempt to establish harmony in the community. But, as I have argued in relation to the mimetic discourses of Greco-Roman antiquity in general, the equations drawn here have far-reaching implications for the questions of social formation and power relations. Sameness, unity, and harmony are to be achieved through imitation; they also circumscribe the community which is unified, in contrast to those who are different. By implication, difference is equated with diffusion, disorder, and discord. So, difference is placed outside of the community, and literally has no place in the community. Any argument against Paul is then cast in these terms: to oppose Paul does not have the status of a mere difference of opinion. Rather, it sets one in opposition to the community, its gospel, and its savior. "Become imitators of me" is a call to sameness which erases difference and, at the same time, reinforces the authoritative status of the model.

In between these two calls to sameness—through the evocation of baptism's unifying qualities and through the exhortation to imitation—lies the rest of Paul's argument against the community's factionalism, which can be divided thematically into three sections. I have adopted Fiore's useful schema for analyzing the structure of these "paradigmatic sections" in accordance with his rhetorical presuppositions (Fiore 1982:315-319). The rhetoric of each of these sections is important, because it reveals the philosophical undergirding of Paul's discourse generally. Each section grounds its argument in simple if harshly drawn contrasts; the resulting stark dualisms reveal the frame of Paul's discourse as one which cannot sustain difference.

The first paradigmatic section, 1:18-2:5, serves to contrast earthly wisdom with the message of Christ crucified. Within this passage, several dualistic oppositions are set up:

those who are perishing (*hoi apollumenoi*)	those who are saved (*hoi sôzomenoi*)
word of the cross as folly (*ho logos ho tou staurou* [*estin*] *môria*)	word of the cross as power of God (*ho logos ho tou staurou* [*estin*] *hê dunamis theou*)
wisdom of the world (*hê sophia tou kosmou*)	power of God (*hê dunamis tou theou*)

foolishness (*to môron*)	wisdom (*hê sophia*)
weakness (*to asthenês*)	strength (*to ischuron*)

These oppositions are ironically articulated, because the things of the world become inverted into powerful attributes for the faithful. While the convert may not have been, by worldly standards, wise, powerful, or of noble birth, these lowly qualities are just those which are transformed by the power of God (1:26-29). This ironic aspect of the dualisms which pervade the letter appears especially in Paul's language about strength and weakness; Paul's self-ascribed weakness is itself a form of power (Schütz 229).

In 1:30, the oscillation between the second-person plural and the first-person plural is a subtle but effective rhetorical move. In 1:26-29, Paul has characterized the community in terms which set it apart from the world. In 1:30, he points out that God has been the source of the community's life in Christ (*ex autou de humeis este en Christô Iêsou*), whom God made "*our* wisdom, *our* righteousness and sanctification and redemption" (*hos egenêthê sophia hêmin apo theou, dikaiosunê te kai hagiasmos kai apolutrôsis*). This shift in person is significant because it subtly reinscribes the connection between Paul and the faithful under the aegis of Christ as wisdom, righteousness, and so on. Paul claims the faithful for his own, marking the boundaries that separate the community from outsiders.

In 2:1-5 Paul employs again the powerful rhetorical argument that he is nothing but a conduit for the demonstration of God's power. Here again, this kind of self-description claims a special, unassailable position from which to speak. Paul does not compete with those whose teachings are by their very nature "the wisdom of men," wisdom which has already been set in opposition to "the power of God." Rather, he sets an example of God's power to which the faithful will be drawn, an example which is empty of any content but that which is inspired by God's power. By casting his position in these terms, Paul has again made himself immune to criticism because he has aligned himself with all of the "positive" elements in the schema sketched out above.

The second section, 2:6-3:5, continues to cast the situation in harshly dualistic terms. The following set of oppositions are set up:

wisdom of this age	wisdom of God
(*hê sophia tou aiônos toutou*)	(*hê sophia theou*)
spirit of the world	spirit which is from God
(*to pneuma tou kosmou*)	(*to pneuma to ek tou theou*)
unspiritual person	spiritual person
(person of the flesh)	
(*psuchikos anthrôpos*)	(*ho pneumatikos*)

Further, Paul describes the Corinthians as babes in Christ (3:1), not ready for solid food (3:2). This characterization of the Corinthians is a pejorative one, reiterating the political nature of the metaphor of the father-child relationship; this is not a reciprocal relationship.

The third section (3:6-4:5) sets up a double comparison. The first comparison is between the work of Paul and the work of Apollos, which Paul constructs as equal (3:8: "He who plants and he who waters are equal," *ho phuteuôn de kai ho potizôn en eisin*). The second comparison is actually a sharp contrast between these apostles' harmony in working together, each doing his own task, and the factionalism in the community. Several things are of note here. First, there is a clear hierarchical separation between the apostles on the one hand and the community on the other expressed in these two comparisons. 1 Cor 3:9 reads, "For we are God's fellow workers; you are God's field, God's building" (*theou gar esmen sunergoi, theou geôrgion, theou oikodomê este*). While Apollos and Paul are the fellow workers of God, the community is characterized as the passive object of that apostolic work. Also, while there is no equality being expressed here, neither is there any expression of reciprocity: the community is the recipient of the apostles' work. Finally, while Apollos is being set up here as a fellow example for the Corinthians, he will be supplanted later, as we shall see, by the singular model of Paul.

1 Cor 4:6-21 is the passage which contains the explicit exhortation to imitate Paul. Its relationship to what has gone before is a much debated exegetical problem. Specifically, debate focuses on various terms in verse 6 which evade obvious explanation. For example, the meaning of *meteschêmatisa* (RSV: "I have applied") is not immediately evident in this context.[13] The figurative sense of *metaschêmatizein* (to transform, to change) has dominated the contemporary scholarly consensus about the usage here, and it is the most sensible possibility: the writer is setting up as figures himself and Apollos *hina en humin mathête* ("in order that you might learn by us," i.e., by means of our example).

Next, scholars have debated the referent of the pronoun *tauta* ("these things"): the term might refer simply to the first five verses in chapter 4 (Craig 1953:54), to the third paradigmatic section (3:6-4:5) (Robertson and Plummer 1914:80; Lietzmann 1923:19), or to the entire argument which precedes (Parry 1916:44; cf. Fiore 1982:321). The first possibility, that *tauta* refers to 4:1-5, is doubtful, since Apollos is not mentioned except generally in the pronoun *hêmas* ("us") in verse 1, and since there is no reason on the basis of structure or content to separate 4:1-5 from the rest of the third section, 3:6-4:5. Clearly, *tauta* refers *at least* to the third paradigmatic section, where Apollos figures prominently. The most compelling argument for the pronoun referring to the entire preceding argument can be made on the basis of rhetoric. The three paradigmatic sections are interlocking and best understood as a piece.

The phrase, *to mê huper ha gegraptai* ("not to go beyond what has been written"), causes considerable difficulty. Most scholars conclude that the phrase cannot be interpreted satisfactorily.[14] At most, what is clear is that Paul and Apollos are both to be seen as figures or models from whom the Corinthians may learn. The object of that learning—*to mê huper ha gegraptai*—is irretrievable.

Verses 8-13 function as a kind of rhetorical crescendo, sharply contrasting the Corinthians on the one hand and Paul (and Apollos?) on the other. The structure of these verses is not precisely chiastic, except in the central verse (vs. 10) (Conzelmann 1975:89). One can observe, however, the clear shift in subject from verse 8, where Paul makes use of sarcasm and irony to characterize the position of those whom he rebukes, to verses 11-13, where "our" sufferings are catalogued. In the midst of this, the oppositions are clearly drawn in verse 10:

we are fools for Christ's sake	you are wise in Christ
(hêmeis môroi dia Christon)	(humeis phronimoi en Christô)
we are weak	you are strong
(hêmeis astheneis)	(humeis ischuroi)
we are held in disrepute	your are held in honor
(hêmeis atimoi)	(humeis endoxoi)

From these oppositions, Paul shifts to a call to become his imitators.

At this juncture there is a sharp transition from the first-person plural to the first-person singular. This is a recurrent problem in Paul's letters as we saw earlier in 1 Thessalonians—where it also had implications for the interpretation of imitation. Although Paul has used Apollos as a co-example in the third paradigmatic section and also in 4:6, he shifts decisively at 4:14-21 to the first-person singular where he both refers to himself as the one father of the community ("For though you have countless guides in Christ, you do not have many fathers. For I became your father in Christ Jesus through the gospel" 4:15) and exhorts the Corinthians to be his imitators (4:16). The force of the *oun* ("therefore") in 4:16 (*Parakalô oun humas, mimêtai mou ginesthe*, "therefore I exhort you: be imitators of me") is inferential, and the exhortation of Paul is grounded in his special status as father.[15] There is a profound tension between the representation of Paul and Apollos as co-workers and equals in 3:6-4:5 (and even through 4:13) on the one hand, and on the other hand, Paul's clear and forceful singular voice in 3:1-4 and 4:14-21. A satisfactory resolution to this tension is not apparent; in fact most commentators are silent on the matter. The exception is Fiore, who argues that the emergence of the singular model/example—Paul—is a logical and self-evident move. The argument moves from the factionalist controversy (where multiple examples relating harmoniously function as an essential counter-example to the problems in the community) to the causes of that controversy (wrong wisdom and judgment) where the single virtuous example is operative.[16]

Two observations emerge in relation to Fiore's argument. First, this shift from a plural to a singular model points to the fact that Paul has set himself up as *the* authoritative speaker and uses the language of mimesis to undergird that privileged position. The shift has implications for the power relations in the community vis-à-vis its leaders. In some ways, Apollos is not equal with Paul if Paul holds the privileged position of the father. Apollos is more nearly equal to Paul than the Corinthians are, but there remains a hierarchy of position. Second, Fiore's argument raises certain questions about power. What are the implications of putting forward a *single* model in the arena of wisdom and judgment? Does this mean that there is but one way to wisdom (truth)? How does this affect power relations in the early Corinthian community? Fiore argues that Paul puts himself forward as an example because he feels a "special responsibility" as the founder of the community, but Fiore does not deal with the political ramifications of this "special responsibility." Ultimately, the other side of "special responsibility" is "special position," "a privileged position from which to speak."

It remains to discuss the content of this imitation of Paul in 4:16ff. Verse 17 has inspired much exegetical debate:

> Therefore I sent to you Timothy, my beloved and faithful child in the Lord, to remind you of my ways in Christ, as I teach them everywhere in every church.

> *Dia touto epempsa humin Timotheon, hos estin mou teknon agapêton kai piston en kuriô, hos humas anamnêsei tas hodous mou tas en Christô, kathôs pantachou en pasê ekklêsia didaskô.*

Michaelis argues that the *kathôs* ("as") clause, in modifying Paul's "ways in Christ" in terms of his general teaching to all the communities, signifies not personal imitation of Paul's example but rather more general obedience to the apostle's command (Michaelis 1967:670). Lietzmann understands "ways in Christ" to mean "general principles" to which the community's behavior should attain (Lietzmann 1923:22), while Wendland attributes to them the idea of Paul's preaching of the gospel and his exhortations to the community (Wendland 1980: 37). Gerhardsson describes them as "an extensive collection of text material the contents of which are primarily ethical and paraenetic in character" (Gerhardsson 1961:294). Conzelmann ties the notion of "ways" specifically to Paul's teaching (Conzelmann 1975:92)[17], and joins de Boer in seeing the background for this notion in the Hebrew Bible (Conzelmann 1975:92 n. 21; de Boer 1962:148-149). Betz observes that "the way" is a technical term from Hellenistic mystery religions, and sees in *hodoi mou hai en Christô* ("my ways in Christ") an expression of the "way" of the pre-existent Christ, as it is described in Phil 2:6ff (Betz 1967:156).

This debate on the actual content of mimesis and Paul's ways in Christ is significant when one considers the political nature of mimesis. That is, one is hard-pressed to produce a univocal, concrete expression of what exactly the Corinthians are being called to imitate. De Boer argues that this lack of specificity is an expression of Paul's gentleness toward the community, and invokes Paul's father image as evidence of this gentleness:

> It is surprising that he has no specific orders to issue to them and no solemn injunctions to place upon them. He does not approach them with a solemn "Thus saith the Lord." Rather, he approaches them as Paul, their friend, their servant, and their father. He seeks to motivate a change in them by an appeal to their personal attachment to him. He sets aside any impulse to command them with apostolic authority. He is determined to exploit to the fullest extent the way of gentleness and love. He is confident that there is still a personal tie between them, and he makes his appeal to them on the basis of this personal tie. As beloved children of your father, be my imitators. (De Boer 1962:152-153)

As we have seen, the paternal metaphor does not necessarily evoke a sense of kindness or love. Further, while Paul may be using his personal relationship with the community in exhorting them to be his imitators, he still appeals to his own authority.

I would hold that the lack of specific content in his exhortation to imitate him reflects an aspect of the political nature of the relationship between him and the community. The call to imitation constructs power relations in the community precisely because of the slipperiness of the object of imitation. Foucault has ably demonstrated in his work on technologies of power how the more generalized and unpredictable the technology's application, the more effective its result.[18] Similarly, if the moral exhortation is generalized, nonspecific, inexact, then the onus is upon the exhorted one to perform correctly. Because the exhortation does not provide specific criteria against which performance can be measured, the one exhorted must always be self-policing. Just as many technologies of power are constructed to create such self-surveillance, so imprecise exhortations to imitate a model have the dual effect of reinscribing the model's authority while placing the imitator in the position of perpetual unease as to whether s/he is acting in the proper mimetic fashion.

Another aspect of this call to imitate and to remember "my ways in Christ" is the peculiar, though not unique, way in which Paul appropriates for himself what one might usually expect to be attributed to Christ or God. In 1 Thessalonians, as we have seen, Paul refers to "our gospel" at one point, and later "Christ's gospel" and "God's gospel."[19] Here, one might well expect to read "Christ's ways" rather than "my ways in Christ," especially if one is to accept Conzelmann's and de Boer's philological conclusions about the parallel between this expression and similar expressions in the Hebrew Bible—where the phrase is "God's ways" (de Boer 1962:149). As with the 1 Thessalonians passages, there exists here a strange confusion on Paul's part about his own role or identity; if he has appropriated the Hebrew Bible's usage of "God's ways," then he is claiming a special status for himself by calling the Corinthians to remember "his ways." By expressing it in the revised form of "my ways in Christ," he furthers the confusion, by claiming authority for himself ("my ways") and shoring it up by tying it to Christ's authority ("in Christ"). At best, there is tension here; at worst, an expression of a deeper confusion about Paul's identity vis-à-vis God and Christ.[20]

To summarize: Paul's double invocation of mimesis language in 1 Corinthians is not fortuitous, but rather is logical in terms of the letter's thematic content. Mimesis is invoked precisely because it is bound up in Paul's discourse with problems of community structure and the authority of leaders, of the community's social identity, of appropriate access to wisdom (correct knowledge) or truth. The call to unity in 1 Cor 1:10-17 and the call to imitation in 4:14-21 reiterate and reinforce one another while rhetorically surrounding a discourse of mimetic examples which build upon one another to create a heightened effect at 4:14-21. The starkly dualistic nature of Paul's rhetoric in the series of mimetic examples has political implications for determining the nature of the mimetic relationship between Paul and the Corinthian community. The political nature of the paternal metaphor that Paul uses often in relation to mimetic language evokes authority, while the imprecise content of mimesis in 1 Cor 4:16 has a political function as well. It reinscribes the authority of the model while forcing the imitators to "police themselves" because the exact nature of what they are called to do is elusive. The confusion of identity noted earlier in 1 Thessalonians expresses itself again in Paul's peculiar formulation, "my ways in Christ," and suggests again the problem of authority. All of these conclusions and nuances of significance echo in Paul's reiteration of the exhortation, *mimētai mou ginesthe* ("be imitators of me"), at 1 Cor 11:1.

1 Corinthians 11:1

The exhortation to become imitators of Paul appears again in 1 Corinthians, at the end of the discussion about eating meat sacrificed to pagan deities (8:1-11:1). Paul's response to the problem is threefold: first, the Christian is free to eat this food, as pagan deities have no power over the Christian (8:1-6); second, the Christian's concern for other Christians might well mediate and limit the person's freedom to do what s/he wishes (8:7-9:17); and third, a certain caution in the face of possible temptation is useful (10:1-13). Paul offers his solution to the problem in the last verses of chapter 10 (10:14-30). Then the exhortation, of which the mimesis passage is a part, appears:

> So, whether you eat or drink, or whatever you do, do all to the glory of God. Give no offense to Jews or Greeks or to the church of God, just as I try to please all men in everything I do, not seeking my own advantage, but that of many, that they may be saved. Be imitators of me, as I am of Christ. (1 Cor 10:31-11:1)

This exhortation can be read as simply a commonsense piece of advice to the Corinthians. The advice that one must not offend Jews or Greeks or others in the Christian community seems quite straightforward. It protects the Christian community from divisions and internal conflicts. However, this is not a sufficient rendering of the passage.

First of all, Paul advocates a particular structure of relationships between himself and the Corinthians on the one hand, and between Christ and himself on the other. He exhorts the Corinthians to become imitators of him "as I am of Christ" (kathōs kagō Christou). The parallelism here cannot go unnoticed (see Stanley 1959:875). Christ is to Paul as Paul is to the Corinthians; Paul asks for an act of imitatio Pauli which mirrors his own imitatio Christi. What exactly is the nature of Paul's imitation of Christ? Some have argued that the object of imitation is the pre-existent Christ rather than the historical Jesus (Bultmann 1933:206; Lietzmann 1923:53; Conzelmann 1975: 180; Schulz 1962:285-289; D. Williams 1967:370-371; de Boer 1962:159); others have insisted that the referent is the historical Jesus (de Boer 1962:159; D. Williams 1967:371-372).[21]

However imitatio Christi is defined, Paul's act of imitation is an act of mediation. But it is also a presumptuous move on Paul's part, because he is setting himself in a structurally similar position to that of Christ.[22] As we have seen in preceding contexts, Paul does appear at times to confuse his own position with that of Christ or God. Here, the call to imitation is interwoven with this confusion of identity.

In addition, this act of mediation presupposes a hierarchical structure: Community/Paul/Christ/God. Paul's demand of imitation here is founded on an idea of non-reciprocity. That is, the community must imitate Paul as Paul must imitate Christ (who, presumably, must imitate God). The lines of relationship move in only one direction. Paul, by acting as intermediary between Christ and the gospel on the one hand, and the community on the other, has constructed a hierarchy which, above all else, undergirds and reinforces his own privileged position. Stanley acknowledges the hierarchical view of imitation here, but tries to cast it in the most positive light:

> There is an essentially hierarchical structure in this Pauline conception of 'imitation', which shows how important he considers his function of transmitting the apostolic faith to others . . . . The Corinthian community is not called upon to imitate Christ directly, but to imitate Paul in whom they possess a concrete realization of the imitation of Christ. By insisting upon this necessarily mediated *imitatio Christi*, Paul is simply witnessing to the necessity of apostolic tradition in the life of the Church. (Stanley 1959:874)

This argument attempts to make the notion of "apostolic tradition" self-evident, implicitly set apart from any question about power relations between the community and its leadership. To place oneself in a line of succession or tradition, as Paul does (and this is reinforced by 11:2 which follows), affects power relations. Paul's claim to a special position vis-à-vis tradition and Christ (in his claim to the position of mediator in the mimetic relationship) has an impact on the construction of power relations in the early communities.

Furthermore, to couch this exhortation in the context of a discussion about community life (that is, about how to sustain a level of communal harmony and identity in the face of potential "outside" threats) is a rhetorically loaded move for Paul. Again, it sets imitation of Paul within the context of creating a community of sameness, and since the exhortation follows the statement that Paul takes every action "trying to please all men in everything I do, not seeking my own advantage, but that of many, that they may be saved," he has set this economy of sameness within the context of salvation. Sameness is not a simple social expediency but is tied to the salvation of the community. By implication, difference is cast in stark contrast to the community's salvation (see Shaw 1983:86).

The discussion of the problem of eating idol meat concerns not the material act itself but what it signifies, both to the agents of the act and to the social group (the Corinthian community) as a whole. In other words, the action itself is not intrinsically dangerous to individuals or the group, which is presumably why Paul does not issue a singular, absolute ruling on the action. Rather, the action becomes dangerous to the group when the "weak" people understand their activity to blur the distinctions between Christian and pagan. The issue really is one of group identity and the setting of boundaries between the group and the rest of the world; the question becomes one of determining the limits of Christian identity in contrast to others (Meeks 1983: 84-94; Guénel 1983).

It is precisely in this sense that the call to imitation in 1 Cor 11:1, tied as it is to the broader concern of determining Christian identity in contrast to the rest of the world, functions as the "underside" of the call to imitation in 1 Cor 4:16. The previous section of this chapter has demonstrated how the call to imitation in 4:16 is tied to the call to unity in the first part of the letter. Here at 11:1, the call to imitation closes a section which deals with questions of exclusivity, or how to tell a Christian from a non-Christian. The call to sameness (with Paul) in 11:1 is paradoxically bound up with the call to exclusivity (difference) from the rest of the world. The action of imitation again has no specified content, but refers rather to a gesture which would set Christians apart as Christians. Unity and exclusivity are two sides of the same coin in the economy of Christian social formation. Each quality is a function of the mimetic relationship, insofar as each is played out in the polarity of sameness and difference. Unity within the Christian community demands sameness within; exclusivity from the rest of the world demands (implicitly) sameness within and difference from without. Both unity and exclusivity depend, finally, in this text, on the mimetic relationship of the community to its model Paul.

Imitation of Paul in both contexts (4:16 and 11:1) has to do fundamentally with the social arrangement of the Corinthian community (unity and identity) and always refers back to the singular authoritative model of Paul. Although the calls to imitation in the two places in the letter have specific functions within the letter's rhetoric, both refer to the necessity of Paul as singular model within the social formation and both are grounded in the valuing of sameness over difference.

Difference, then, plays a paradoxical role in determining social boundaries. That is to say, difference operates at the level of determining social boundaries only in a negative sense. Difference is necessary in order to define the "same;" "others" are necessary in order to invent the "self." The concept of difference functions here only to invent and imbue with value the concept of the same. Christians are called in this letter to imitate (to be the same as) Paul while their difference from the rest of the world is continually articulated as their salvation. It is perhaps better seen in this way: it is the Christians' sameness that is their salvation, while it is the non-Christians' difference that is their damnation. Paul's call to imitation has a socially expedient function to be sure, but it also possesses a more profound level of meaning because the imitation of Paul's example is itself a privileged mode of access to salvation.

A NOTE ON GALATIANS 4:12

The call in Gal 4:12 to "become as I am, for I also have become as you are" is generally taken to reflect Paul's mimetic discourse, despite the absence of the technical term itself.[23] Without going into detail, let me make a few observations.

The verse is perhaps more confusing for its apparent parallelism: "Brethren, I beseech you, become as I am, for I also have become as you are" (*Ginesthe hôs egô, hoti kagô hôs humeis, adelphoi, deomai humôn*). De Boer's reading of the text is the most compelling. He argues that the parallelism is, in fact, only apparent. Paul's action of forsaking the law had the *result* of Paul becoming like the Gentiles, but the action was not motivated by any *intention* to become like the Gentiles. The reverse is not the case; the Gentiles are called upon to free themselves from the law, and to do so by becoming like Paul (de Boer 193). Paul and the Galatians do not function as mutual or reciprocal models; Paul remains the privileged model for the community he addresses.

Paul again invokes the imagery of fatherhood in this passage. The political nuances of this image have already been noted, and this passage only reiterates the ambiguous nature of the image and strengthens the argument put forward in relation to 1 Cor 4:16. Earlier in Galatians 4, Paul uses the metaphor of childhood to illustrate a point about status:

> I mean that the heir, as long as he is a child, is no better than a slave, though he is the owner of all the estate; but he is under guardians and trustees until the date set by the father. So with us; when we were children, we were slaves to the elemental spirits of the universe. (Gal 4:1-3)

The hierarchical nature of the father-child relationship is clearly invoked in these verses; the father image remains compellingly linked with the idea of imitation.

The larger context of the call to "become as I am" is, of course, the nature of the Galatians' practice in relation to the law. Here, the force of "become as I am" echoes the exhortations elsewhere, "become imitators of me." Both function as a call to sameness with its implicit indictment of difference.

CONCLUSIONS

Paul's discourse of mimesis uses rhetoric to rationalize and shore up a particular set of social relations or power relations within the early Christian movement. His use of the notion of mimesis, with all of its nuances, reinforces both Paul's own privileged position and the power relations of the early Christian communities as somehow "natural." That is to say, the hierarchy of power is in tune with a much larger and more self-evident structure which incorporates both the earthly community and the divine order. Participating positively in the mimetic relationship with Paul, the early communities are to be rewarded with salvation. Resisting the mimetic relationship, by contrast, has dire consequences.

Paul's invocation of mimesis indicts the very notion of difference, and thereby constructs the nature of early Christian social relationship: Christians are Christians insofar as they strive for the privileged goal of sameness. Christians distinguish themselves from those who are not Christians, who are not saved, precisely in this drive for sameness. Difference has only negative connotations in this mimetic economy.

Furthermore, the privileged position of the model in the mimetic relationship has far-reaching implications for the nature of early Christian power relations: *mimēsis Paulou* is no simple case of emulating a benign ethical model, and cannot be condensed to refer to a self-evident social pragmatism. Rather, its dependence on the ideology of mimesis suggests that it has a much more profound significance, that it constructs the early communities within a hierarchical economy of sameness which both appropriates the members of the early communities and reinscribes Paul's privileged position as natural. It is at the level of this kind of social effect of the rhetoric of Paul's discourse that the nature of mimesis in early Christian discourse can be seen in clearest terms, as a reinscription of imposed power relations as natural within the emerging social formation of early Christianity.

5

READING EFFECTS: IMITATION, POWER, AND CLAIMS TO TRUTH

The erasure of difference through the call to imitation is, as we have seen, a pragmatic and conceptual part of Paul's consolidation of his apostolic authority. By promoting the value of sameness he is also shaping relations of power. The effects of his rhetorical gesture to erase difference are not limited, however, to Paul's first-century readers—a series of tiny Christian enclaves tucked in the midst of communities with which they were sometimes quite at odds. For, of course, the letters have also been delivered to destinations far beyond the first-century Mediterranean basin. That Paul's letters were so quickly collected, circulated, and indeed imitated, complicates and broadens any discussion of the effects of his discourse. Further, insofar as this writing the history of mimesis is, in Foucault's language, "writing the history of the present," it is crucial that we think beyond the first century and look at the reading effects of Paul's discourse in our own context, Western culture in the late twentieth century. The Bible, into which Paul's occasional letters were woven, is obviously a major source for the master narratives that have constructed Western culture. Even now, twenty centuries and a number of major epistemic shifts later, the effects of these biblical texts continue to modulate and reverberate culturally.

Foucault urges us to look back into history to moments when the categories we take for granted were strange and new. We ought not trace the "origins" of ideology in some simple fashion, but rather we ought to begin to think about the contingency of what appears "natural" in our culture—or better, what does not appear at all, because it has become so thoroughly part of our unspoken and unthought cultural landscape. In Paul's discourse of mimesis I see one strand of a more complex weave that has contributed to the cultural landscape of the West—what I have called earlier in this volume "the economy of sameness" or, following Biddy Martin's formulation, "the hegemony of the identical." Implicit in my reading of Paul's language of mimesis has been a critique of the economy of sameness. I wish now to develop that critique more explicitly by elaborating theoretically its effects. I draw on diverse discourses of the last twenty years or so by cultural critics who have helped lay bare the contingencies and limitations of Western modes of knowledge and social formation.

First, however, there is a crucial issue I need to address, namely the issue of intentionality. Whether Paul *meant* or *intended* that his discourse be understood in the way I have argued is not a question that I have answered. Indeed, for methodological and hermeneutical reasons, I have bracketed the whole matter of conscious authorial intent. I assume here that the author's intent—the motive residing in the mind of the writer—is unattainable because it involves inaccessible aspects of the author's psychology. In any case, to assume that verbal expression is continuous with authorial intent is to assume that language is transparent and self-evident, a conduit of communication which leaves no remainder. Such an assumption contradicts almost all but the most romantic philosophies of language and theories of linguistic expression. Theory has demonstrated the slipperiness of every linguistic expression—the gap between intent and effect, the semiotic notion of sliding signification.[1]

To assert that "Paul did not mean that," in relation to this reading, is therefore irrelevant. I have produced my readings from two grounds: the rhetorical character of the texts themselves, and the larger textual world of which they are a part and on which they consciously or unconsciously draw. The significance of mimesis in that larger textual world has been made clear: one cannot read "mimesis" in Paul outside of this framework, even allowing for the particularity of a specific discourse.

At the same time, I stress that my reading is not the only possible or plausible one. Like all readers, I have focused on particular questions and issues which strike me as especially salient, and I have framed my discussion according to my interests. In some quarters, such a statement may well appear as a defensive admission, but I do not see it this way. Because my reading is framed by my interests it is not therefore capricious, idiosyncratic, or absolutely subjective (unrepeatable and utterly perspectival and relative). Rather, it is (like any other) simply not a totalizing one; it does not claim to stand as the singularly true reading of Paul's discourse. Clearly, certain aspects of Paul's texts strike me as particularly relevant and interesting, and I have pursued them by a reading strategy that another reader could well adopt. But the point here is that my reading is possible, plausible, and I hope also persuasive; it illuminates in a new way certain features of the text, and raises questions that have not until now been explored fully. By focusing on the effects of reading rather than on the author's intentions, I have joined those biblical critics who have been shifting the terms of the discussion, asking readers to pose questions of meaning from a different point of view from the one often taken in biblical studies. My line of inquiry is meant to be both provocative and illuminating, looking at the text not simply as a historical artifact from a period quite removed from our own (and the questions that concern our own period of history), but as a continuously-producing source of meanings as timely and urgent now as at first writing.

IMITATION AND PAUL'S PASTORAL POWER

The theoretical discussion of Foucault's analytics of power drew attention to the elements he argued were necessary for creating and sustaining power relations. These elements were: (1) the *system of differentiations* enabling the hierarchical relationship between dominant and subordinate to be continually enacted, a creation of structures of "self" and "other"; (2) some articulated *types of objectives* held by those who act upon others; (3) some identifiable *means* for bringing these relationships into being; (4) social structures through which power circulates, or in Foucault's language, *forms of institutionalization*; and (5) some mode of *rationalization* of the relations of power (Foucault 1982:223). It is not difficult to see these elements present in Pauline discourse (both in general and in the language of imitation in particular) and in the relationships constructed between the apostle and early Christian communities.

At first glance it might seem ironic to argue that Paul's pastoral power, as it is expressed in his exhortations to sameness, is grounded in a system of differentiations, an articulation of self and other. But where Paul uses the idea of imitation, this is noticeably so, particularly where his own apostolic person is contrasted with other possible models. Blurred distinctions occur when identity shifts between the first-person singular and the first-person plural, and Paul's audience is never included in the reference to "us." Further, differentiation also continues to qualify the mimetic relationship insofar as Paul continuously attributes superior value to the superordinate figure (the self, Paul), even while exhorting the subordinate figure (the other, the imitator) to obliterate its difference. Finally, as will become clearer below, the valorization of sameness always already presupposes difference as its source. Therefore, where imitation is concerned, Paul's pastoral power is grounded in the hierarchy that differentiates the apostle's position from that of the nascent communities.

Paul's pastoral power, articulated in his discourse and situated in a system of differentiation, has explicit objectives: to attempt to solve particular community problems, to (re)authorize

122

his own teachings and the people whom he sends in his place, to assure that the communities follow a particular pattern in living out their new Christian self-understanding, and ultimately to guarantee their claims to salvation. These objectives layer the social, individual, and spiritual planes of existence; each implicates the other, and situates Paul's pastoral power simultaneously on the multiple levels.

Clearly the most powerful means at Paul's disposal for creating his relationships of power with his communities are ideological. After all, he does not possess any special physical means to coerce people to relate to him in a certain way; and he has no state apparatus (police or military) to ensure compliance. Nor obviously would I argue that he actively coerces people against their conscious wills to place themselves in a subordinate relationship to him. Rather he is attempting to persuade them by two simultaneous means—rhetoric and personal authority. The effectiveness of these means must be measured by the degree to which they make what Paul claims to be true appear actually to be true and render other competing claims to truth impossible or unthinkable. The close readings in the last chapter spelled out how the intersections of rhetoric and apostolic authority (idioms of kinship and hierarchy—sameness and difference—and claims to special status) were at the heart of the exhortation of imitation and became part of Paul's ability to assert a claim to pastoral power.

The institutional location of Paul's pastoral power is a problem when using Foucault's model to help understand the language of imitation, since the institutional shape of "the church" in large measure remains amorphous for at least a generation or two after Paul's activity.[2] Nevertheless, Paul uses the language of *ekklēsia* when addressing his communities and presupposes recognizable structures even if they are rather malleable social networks at this point. Further, his deployment of the idiom of kinship (positioning himself as the father of his communities) calls up the analogous institution of the family with its fairly firmly entrenched internal power relations. Certainly, institutional location is the weakest link in the use of Foucault's model, though this is not surprising given that

Paul's power is ideological rather than material, located in discourse more than in institutional formations in this early period.

Our object of analysis has been, throughout, the ways in which relations of power have been rationalized, and these modes of rationalization need no further elaborating. The intersections of Paul's rhetorical gestures and claims to personal authority, theological arguments and attacks on his opponents form a complex matrix of rationalization of power relations constructed by the discourse of imitation. The continuing effects of this construct of power are what remain to be explored.

READING MIMESIS OTHERWISE OR, WHAT'S THE DIFFERENCE?

What are the broader implications of reading Paul's powerful discourse of mimesis as a demand for the erasure of difference? We have already seen what this reading might mean for reconstructing a picture of early Christian social formation. More broadly, what might it mean for thinking about the constructions of Christianity more generally? The answers to these questions fall into several general categories. The first of these is *the problem of sameness and difference*, or what the "economy of sameness" and "hegemony of the identical" imply for Christian discourse. This discussion points in turn to *the problem of universalism* implicit in claims of sameness. Some have argued, further, that the exhortation to sameness is merely a *political strategy*, a necessary maneuver in the process of creating a lasting tradition. This argument requires some engagement. All these issues lead finally to a discussion of *the question of power and claims to truth.*

Sameness and Difference

Paul's discourse of imitation contributes, I have argued, to a broader valorization of sameness and the concomitant repression of difference. Western culture embraces identity and sameness while it rejects difference, which is generally figured either as the failure to achieve identity or as a threatening challenge to identity. Calls to rethink this hierarchical and dualistic arrangement of the categories of sameness and difference (of self and other) have emerged from various quarters in recent years, some challenging the dualism on philosophical grounds, others on political grounds. The most thoroughgoing philosophical challenge to this system of value emerges from the work of French philosopher Jacques Derrida, whose critiques of the Western metaphysics of presence, logocentrism, and the self-presence of truth have refocused much of this generation's discussion of texts and the production of meanings. I do not undertake to elaborate Derrida's complex body of work here, but rather to point to some of its implications for the present inquiry.[3]

Derrida's project of deconstruction aims at unveiling the rhetorical structures that have constructed Western philosophy's devaluation of the notion of "writing." This devaluation is, to Derrida's way of thinking, not at all capricious, but rather reflects a larger interest that might well be named the desire for the mastery of truth. This desire for mastery is expressed in the omnipresence in Western thought of conceptual binary oppositions, dualistic partners that are not equal, symmetrical, or complementary. These dualistic partners are not meant to constitute a whole, but rather are hierarchically paired with one privileged element and one degraded or devalued element. It is not difficult to make a list of such pairs from the common parlance of Western cultural discourse: God/humanity, spirit/body, life/death, man/woman, presence/absence, being/nonbeing, speech/writing, identity/difference. Each of the privileged elements relates to the other privileged elements in a kind of natural relation; speech is related to spirit to being to presence to God. Writing in this arrangement is always construed as a simple, degraded representation of speech; it is related in its essence to materiality, death, absence, nonbeing. The result of deconstructive practice, Derrida asserts, is not to privilege the once devalued term, not to invert the hierarchy, but to undercut the system that constructs the hierarchy, by unveiling the illusion of purity with which the first term is imbued:

> Writing is the dissimulation of the natural, primary, and immediate presence of sense to the soul within the logos. Its violence befalls the soul as unconsciousness. Deconstructing this tradition will therefore not consist of reversing it, of making writing innocent. Rather of showing why the violence of writing does not *befall* an innocent language. (Derrida 1976:37)

What has Derrida's argument about writing to do with the language of imitation in Paul's letters? The normative Western claim is that completeness and identity reside in the dominant elements in the hierarchically arranged pairings (speech, being, presence, and so on). The Derridean position argues, in opposition, that these privileged elements are constituted only in relationship to their "opposites." The truth claims of the dominant philosophical system—on behalf of the dominant elements—work only to the extent that the second elements (and by implication, difference itself) are repressed. At the same time, Derrida argues that identity itself is constituted only through difference, that the self-sameness of the positive element is made possible only through its relationship to its already-existent "opposite." It is in this way that identity is decentered within Derridean discourse.

Derrida's argument, ultimately, is against the nostalgic longing for a pristine origin of truth and the desire to return to some primordial unity or sameness. It is an argument against centric notions altogether, insofar as they underwrite the repression of the margins. For the discourse of imitation, the implications of such an argument should be clear. The discourse of imitation participates in this logocentric drive toward the originary unity, repressing as it does so the nagging difference always already implied in the mimetic relationship. Imitation would not be required if difference were not the already existing prior circumstance. The circumstances enveloping the exhortation to imitation—the existence of difference—deconstruct the assertion and valorization of sameness embodied in the exhortation itself.

The most forceful political critiques of this hierarchical system of value have emerged from cultural criticism—especially feminist and post-colonial criticisms.[4] In these discourses, the tensive nature of difference has been foregrounded with nuance and sophistication. The problem might be summarized in this way: traditionally, non-dominant people (women, and colonized and racially marginalized men) have been constructed as the Other by the dominant culture. Without legitimate claims to identity (read: sameness) within the dominant culture, they/we are relegated to the margins of the culture. According to this mode of organizing the world conceptually and socially, one has only two options: to become the same or to be marginalized. (The problem of identity-as-sameness versus identity-as-difference has, in large measure, stymied even oppositional discourses, such as feminist theory. Sameness and difference operate here only as two sides of the same coin, as part of an either/or relationship. The discursive limit this conceptual impasse represents will be discussed in the final section.)

But even as this opposition of same/other has been constituted, the vibrant political and cultural work of the so-called "marginal" resists any construction that denies access to identity and agency. It insists, by a redefinition of the terms, on the legitimacy of their/our claims to *identity in their/our difference*. In other words, power need not be rendered accessible only through becoming the same. At the same time, crucial theoretical questions emerge. What is at stake in attempting to claim an identity-in-difference? Is it a reification of difference, or can it function to undercut the economy of sameness and the hegemony of the identical? Can it, in other words, deconstruct the dominant order?[5]

As we read of sameness and difference in texts which belong to one of the master narratives of Western culture, we encounter these same wide-ranging implications. If my reading of Paul's rhetoric is plausible—that it underwrites sameness and thereby participates in the active repression of difference—then it is reasonable to see Paul's rhetoric as contributing to the broader Western enactment of sameness and resistance to difference. This double move, as I have argued, is not only conceptual or theoretical, but also tied to the social arrangements by which authority becomes located in the person (or group) who embodies sameness. Valuing sameness is not a mere philosophical preference, but a gesture which inscribes certain relations of power. Given the eventual normative status of Paul's rhetoric, the authoritative resonance of the valorization of sameness in his discourse only increases, silencing over time any competing discourses. Further, the power relations the normative discourse underwrites also gain authority and force. As sameness is elevated to the status of a norm, certain relations of power are also lent normative status, and the question arises whether Christian discourse can engage meaningfully identity-in-difference. In other words, how would Christian discourse engage the political critique of the sameness-difference dichotomy? Is it capable of doing so?

Universalism and its Dangers

Historically, one of the ways in which Christian discourse has responded to the problem of sameness-difference is through a tendency toward universalization and a related drive to produce a univocal truth. Obviously, this tendency has far-reaching implications for the question of whether Christianity itself can sustain difference. The argument that the problem of sameness-difference is not really a problem, because of Christianity's (self-proclaimed) universal potential, begs the question of difference altogether and leaves wide open the underside of the asserted universal potential, namely its colonizing potential.

Post-colonial theorists (as well as some feminists) have deconstructed universalism in general, demonstrating the potentially imperialist effects of subsuming diversities and differences under the umbrella of a totalizing sameness. Patronizing notions such as "anonymous Christianity" are only the more blatant results of subsuming variety into a Christian sameness. In the history of evangelizing and missionizing activity, moreover, it is easy to see ways in which the underside of Christian universalism can operate as a (sometimes violent) silencing of divergent voices.[6] (This silencing, it should be said, is quite often no mere figurative gesture, but a real acting out of technologies of power upon human bodies.)

Hand in hand with universalism is the drive within Christian discourse toward claims to univocal truth. Paul's rhetoric makes these kinds of claims again and again, and while they may be read as responses to particular circumstances in which Paul's understanding of Christian meanings was being challenged by alternatives, these situational arguments are also tied to broader theological understandings. Linking particular social configurations to both the truth of Paul's gospel and to the very possibility of salvation broadens the effect of the rhetoric significantly. It then delegitimizes any other possible social forms, paths to salvation, and claims to truth. In short, there is Paul's truth, or there is no truth.

It is not my purpose here to trace out the full effects of the embrace of identity and sameness through the universalist gestures and claims to univocal truth, thereby uncovering some new "truth" about Christian discourse. Rather, I would simply point out that such discourse has produced *multiple effects* resonating and echoing through different historical settings and moments, effects that must be claimed as effects of Christian discourse. Whatever else the tendency toward universalization means—along with the silencing of difference through the assertion of univocal truths—it also implies these problematic effects. Usually in discussion of Christian discourse these tend to be elided or deemphasized. Such minimizing is strikingly dangerous and irresponsible. Whether Christian discourse can disentangle itself from these problematic claims remains an open question, ripe for further debate.

Sameness as Political Strategy: Egalitarianism, the Elision of Differences, and Unity

Some have argued that in Pauline discourse the elision of differences is primarily a move toward constructing an egalitarian social arrangement among early Christian communities. Alternately some might argue further that Paul's exhortation to sameness merely responds to or enacts a crucial social necessity, namely, social identity and community unity in the face of stringent political opposition. Both of these arguments are important ones, and need to be engaged in turn.

My reading of the drive toward reinscribing sameness in Paul's discourse stands over against, or at least in tension with, arguments frequently put forward that Paul advocates breaking down boundaries and creating a new, egalitarian community devoid of hierarchical social arrangements. Rom 12:4-8, 1 Cor 12:4-31, and Gal 3:28 are generally the prooftexts for this position. Such arguments tend to draw attention to Paul's use of the image of the body of Christ to demonstrate that each individual has a particular role to play in the formation of the whole body. This corporate image has dominated Western understandings of social formation and role differentiation at least since Aristotle, who, for his part, acknowledged the hierarchical nature of the differences among the individual constituents of the whole, as in his characterization of the state found in his *Politics*:

> Again, the state, as composed of unlikes, may be compared to the living being: as the first elements into which a living being is resolved are soul and body, as soul is made up of rational principle and appetite, the family of husband and wife, property of master and slave, so of all these, as well as other dissimilar elements, the state is composed; and therefore the excellence of all the citizens cannot possibly be the same, any more than the excellence of the leader of a chorus is the same as that of the performer who stands by his side. (Arist., *Pol.* 1277A)

This organic model not only inscribes a naturalness within socially-constituted relations, it also implies that social order is self-evidently a unity, a closed system with no loose ends, no remainder. However, no social formation begins as a systemic or structural unity. Rather, it originates in a confluence of interests and desires, drives and goals, as was discussed in chapter two (see also Mann 1986:1-2). The question, then, must be posed as follows. Was there an inherent reason why the early Christian movements needed to develop ultimately into a singular, unitary, and monolithic utopian picture of singular salvation? Is this drive toward a unitary, transcendent ideological focus coterminous with the Christian message in particular?

However one might choose to answer that question, two things are clear. First, this drive toward the transcendent ideological focus is located within the movement toward institutionalization, toward a monolithic structure with a singular truth attached. Second, this is a movement that always has to do with power, not simply cosmic power or supernatural power, but power relations negotiated and struggled over in very human social networks. It is this incipient movement toward institutionalization that one observes in Paul's rhetoric, where ideological power is brought to bear in a social setting to produce a particular end: the unity and harmony in the early Christian communities which are a kind of condensed analogy for the more general universalization of Christian discourse. Early Christian movements, without the powerful gestures of writers like Paul, might well have been sustained without the movement toward structure and truth, though they probably would not have been able to continue the development toward cultural hegemony as the centuries passed. Paul's position "worked," in this sense, in creating part of the ground for Christian hegemony in the West.

However, the image of Paul as the quintessential pragmatist remains problematic. The argument that Paul was far-sighted in his vision—that he knew, somehow, that his discourse must be structured in a way to promote this kind of universalism—is difficult to sustain, because it is based on the theological assumption that Christianity's cultural hegemony—Christian civilization—is somehow a natural and necessary product of the social evolution toward ever higher forms of religiosity and social formation. For one thing, the evolutionary model has been abandoned in explanations of the development of society and cultural forms; for another, one can ask on what grounds any claims are made for the necessity of Christianity, as well as question the cost of Christian cultural hegemony, even if such questions remain answerable only obliquely.

The argument concerning political expediency—that the exhortation to imitation is a defensive call to unity within a marginalized and embattled community—raises the important question of social effect, albeit somewhat differently from the way I have framed this issue. To get a social movement going, the argument runs, everyone in the group must pull together, be of one mind, embrace a group identity. Failure to do so is sure to result in diffused energies, confusion, and the eventual unravelling of the group's cohesion. This argument is a variation on the theme voiced by mainstream institutions and powers on a regular basis: the needs and desires of a whole variety of constituencies are unproblematically represented by the needs and desires of the whole. When there are particular interests articulated by a smaller group within the whole, these tend to be relegated to the pejorative category, "special interest," or set aside until the larger agenda of the whole has been attended to.[7] When this argument for unity within a marginalized group is made, it has a certain basic existential appeal. Anyone who has worked on a committee, tried to reach group consensus, or participated in any kind of group activity where a variety of viable and strongly-held opinions have simultaneously held sway can nod sympathetically in assent to this argument. At the same time, it is an argument that refuses to acknowledge certain other dimensions of the call to group unity. Generally speaking, even within a politically marginal group, it is usually those who are in the relatively dominant position who are the most vocal advocates for unity within the group. The argument for unity, in other words, often only masks the interestedness of the positions held by the dominant members of the group. Group unity rewrites the perspective of the dominant in the group as the perspective of the entire group; competing discourses are replaced by a univocal discourse.

There is a second problem with the argument that the call to imitation and sameness is merely a politically expedient call for social unity: it ignores the the fact that Paul's discourse is embedded within a broader theological framework. Paul's own discourse never makes the argument that imitation will simply make things easier for the fledgling Christian communities in relation to a hostile environment. Rather, as we have seen, it ties imitation and the Christian identity formed by the act of imitation to the salvation of individual Christians. Therefore, the expediency argument is reductionist and fails to account for the ideological dimensions of Paul's discourse.

Finally, the argument about unity simply reinscribes the system of meaning that is subject to critique here. The privileging of identity is simply turned on its head, and unity—even that called for within a political context of relative subordination—becomes simply another tyranny of the identical.

Sameness, the Question of Power, and Claims to Truth

> Identity as understood in the context of a certain ideology of dominance has long been a notion that relies on the concept of an essential, authentic core that remains hidden to one's consciousness and requires the elimination of all that is considered foreign or not true to the self, that is to say, not-I, other. In such a concept the other is almost unavoidably either opposed to the self or submitted to the self's dominance. It is always condemned to remain its shadow while attempting to be its equal. (Trinh 1988:71)

> In difference is the irretrievable loss of the illusion of the one. (Haraway 1988:123)

Here in her article, "Not You/Like You: Post-Colonial Women and the Interlocking Question of Identity and Difference," filmmaker and cultural critic Trinh T. Minh-Ha addresses the complex situation confronting post-colonial women, the tensions of same/not same. Her analysis, on the face of it so removed from the arena of Pauline discourse, nevertheless suggests what positions are possible in a mimetic economy of sameness: opposition or submission, shadowy approximations never achieving the status of identity.

The matrix of linked meanings in Paul's discourse of imitation—sameness, proper positioning in relationship to authority and truth, concomitant attention to particular assertions of power—frames Christian identity in the Pauline communities and constitutes otherness/difference/falsehood. Insofar as the Pauline discourse contributes to the broader master narratives of the West, this matrix of meanings calls for certain relationships of power and understandings of truth. Foucault reminds us

133

that power and truth constitute and reinforce each other and in so doing render impossible other relationships of power and understandings of truth. The Pauline drive toward sameness, identity, and a particular understanding of truth reinscribes the relations of power in early Christian communities and renders impossible competing interpretations of power and truth.

What I hope for is to complicate the call to sameness in the text, not in order ultimately to invert the opposition (sameness/difference) but to reinscribe difference as itself a multiplicity constituted by both similarities and differences. Insistence upon sameness and identity at this historical moment may of course be read in numerous ways, but probably cannot help but be read politically. We occupy a historical moment when the West claims to have won the day, when "the end of history" has been brazenly proclaimed in a kind of apocalyptic Hegelian reprise, when the arrogant economy of sameness elides differences seemingly everywhere—most visibly, perhaps, in the arena of global consumerism. At the same time, cultural articulations contradicting the idea that Western hegemony is self-evident, questioning the proclaimed success of the teleological project, and challenging the assertion of sameness have also never been so eloquent or vibrant. So I write out of the recognition that the hegemony of the identical is a highly contested structure of power and also an ongoing theoretical problem, not a problem to be solved by the panacea *difference*, which as soon as it is reified becomes itself another problem; but a problem to be engaged seriously at the level of its lived effects, most notably its political effects.

Reinscribing difference—diffusing the question of identity through multiple differences—remains the next, if almost unthinkable, step in Western (Christian) culture, a culture that has reached certain limits through its continued allegiance to totalizing positions and unproblematized notions of identity. In other words, I am arguing that Christian discourse is radically overextended in the arena of identity, creating a whole range of problems.[8] This is not to cast "blame" on Christian discourse, for the conceptual impasse of the sameness-difference problematic is, in large measure, the inevitable product of Western "duopoly," the dominance of the binary structures that frame conventional thought in the West.[9] This is true, not only for dominant discourses, but for oppositional ones such as "feminism," as well.[10] However, when combined with what Trinh Minh-Ha has named "homocentrism" (Trinh 1989:52), a reigning ideology of the same in which the study of the other is only of interest for what light it sheds on the self, the Western duopoly renders difference only as a shadowy opposite, like the image found on a photographic negative. Reinscribing differences would be a double project of undercutting this derivative character of difference while at the same time forever problematizing the claims of the same to self-identity.

Reinscribing differences is not a project of unproblematic pluralism; nor would it be a version of the curricular vogue, "multi-culturalism," whose noble impulses are more often than not betrayed by the typical strategy, "Add the 'other' and stir"; nor yet a new-and-improved ecumenism. It is not the process of arranging multiple, separate, self-contained identities on a cafeteria buffet, available now for selection as part of one's minimum daily requirement of otherness. Nor is it, to choose another alimentary metaphor, the process of blending multiple components of varying textures and colors into an undifferentiated homogeneous sauce: what Cheryl Kirk-Duggan has wonderfully characterized as cultural mayonnaise—creamy, smooth, and just slightly off-white.[11] Reinscribing differences cannot occur without an adequate analysis of structures of domination and relationships of power, and their connections to the ongoing shapings of identities.

Taking up the task of radically rethinking the categories of identity and difference is a risky venture. It explodes most of the dominant categories we conventionally use for making sense of the world. It brings us very quickly to the limits of both our disciplines and our discourses. I am all too aware of the ways this chapter will be read, for example, as an unexpected detour from the conventional project of reading early Christian texts, even as I am convinced that the texts indicate this theoretical path. And I am more convinced that failure to undertake the risky venture leaves us caught in the snare of the sameness-difference problematic, trapped by endless repetition. I have attempted to read the resonances and effects of one of the contributing strands of that problematic, and to begin to point beyond it. What lies ahead is the work, at once analytical and imaginative, of trying to think differences differently.

NOTES

BIBLIOGRAPHY

INDEXES

NOTES

NOTES TO INTRODUCTION

1. There are many works on this subject, the most important being: Auerbach 1953; Agacinski, Derrida, Kofman, Lacoue-Labarthe, Nancy, Pautrat 1975; Girard 1978; Lyons and Nichols 1982; Morrison 1982; Spariosu 1984.

NOTES TO CHAPTER 1
IMITATION AND PROBLEMS OF
POWER, IDEOLOGY, AND INTERPRETATION

1. Briefly, the scholarly discussion of imitation in the New Testament in general and in Paul's letters in particular may be schematized as follows. First are studies of the notion of "following Jesus" in the gospel traditions (see Aerts 1966; Kittel 1964). Related are studies that focus more generally on the notion of *imitatio Christi* (Lohse 1957-65; Lofthouse 1953-54; Nielen 1938; Schoeps 1950:286-301; Tinsley 1960). Another group of studies addresses points of continuity and discontinuity between the ideas of following and imitating, and these works are the most important and relevant for my inquiry (Michaelis 1967; Betz 1967; de Boer 1962; Larsson 1962; Schulz 1962; D. Williams 1967). Imitation in the Pauline tradition, without concern for these comparative questions, is the subject of several shorter studies (Fiore 1982:304-355; Proudfoot 1963; Sanders 1981; Stanley 1959). Related to these are works concerned primarily with apostolic tradition which discuss imitation as part of that larger concern (Hainz 1972:295-310; Roloff 1965:116-120; Schütz 1975; Holmberg 1980; Petersen 1985). Finally, various monographs on New Testament ethics include an examination of the notion of imitation (Merk 1968:88, 128-131, 190-193; Furnish 1968:218-227; Schnackenburg 1965:42-53, 161-167; Cerfaux 1954:141-143, 283-289; Cerfaux 1962:288-289; Thysman 1966).

2. Schoeps' "history of religions" work attempts to tie the idea of following Jesus to the rabbinic notion of *imitatio dei* (Schoeps 1950; see also Nielen 1938). Specifically, Schoeps claims that Mt 5:48 ("You,

therefore, must be perfect, as your heavenly Father is perfect") is connected to Lev 19:2 ("Say to all the congregation of the people of Israel, You shall be holy; for I the Lord your God am holy"). He argues further that the Pauline use of *mimêsis* is an echo of the call to follow Jesus; that is, he argues for continuity between the gospel and epistolary traditions, and then ties both to what he sees as an earlier Hebrew notion of *imitatio dei*. The difficulty here is twofold. First, later scholarship has demonstrated that the idea of following God is quite absent from the New Testament (Betz 1967:141 n. 6; Schulz 1962:17). Second, as the discussion in chapter three of this study should make clear, the notion of following God or imitating God has its roots in Greek concepts, and it is only when the Hebrew Bible is read through the lens of Greek thinking that one finds any clear reference to *imitatio dei* in those texts (see Betz's critique in 1967:142).

3. Tinsley 1960:138: "The imitation of Christ is the means whereby the Christian participates in and makes his [sic] own the saving events of the 'Way' of Israel which had been uniquely summed up and transformed in Christ."

4. These questions of continuity in the tradition between "following Jesus" (*akolouthein Iêsou*) and "imitation of Paul" (*mimêsis Paulou*) are addressed also in Larsson 1962; Schulz 1962; Betz 1967.

5. Michaelis goes on to argue that it is only in the passages in which he has identified the connection between mimesis and obedience (1 Cor 4:16, 11:1; 1 Thess 1:6; he also includes Eph 5:1, which I have excluded as a deutero-Pauline text) that "Christ and God [are] associated with Paul as authorities in relation to whom one must be a *mimêtes*" (Michaelis 1967:672).

Michaelis has been critiqued primarily by Catholic scholars, who see his insistent reading as grounded in a confessional difference with Catholic spirituality rather than as an exegetically justifiable position (Stanley 1959:861 n. 3 and 862 n. 1; see also Fiore 1982:306-312). Michaelis has made a harsh distinction between the obedience of an authority on the one hand and the imitation of an exemplary model on the other. This is clear throughout his article. Thus, to take but one example, he writes concerning 1 Cor 11:1: "Certainly 11:1 does not refer to examples to be emulated, let alone to models to whom one is to become similar or equal by imitation, but to authorities whose command and admonition are to be obeyed" (669). What is not clear is why these two possible interpretations must be set in such harsh contrast. A more complex rendering of the texts might suggest that there exists a tension in the very notion of mimesis between these two aspects, that mimesis consists of both the emulative and the authoritative. This is one place in which Michaelis' argument falls short, that is, in his insistence on rendering mimesis as a univocal expression of obedience over against all other possible explanations, such as the possibility that the authoritative is interwoven together with the emulative, giving each aspect more rhetorical power.

6. De Boer 1962:206. He emphasizes that the call to imitation is expressed only in letters addressed to communities which Paul founded himself. This point is also stressed by Stanley 1959:877.

7. See for example de Boer 1962:208-209: "We have seen repeatedly how Paul is urging the imitation of himself in the face of outright heretical teachings being propagated among his readers. This was obviously the case in Corinth, Philippi, and Galatia; even in Thessalonica Paul found it necessary to point out the difference between himself and some other teachers who were surely not representing the same gospel as Paul." Also note de Boer's language at pp. 208-209 nn. 13 and 14, where taking a position different from Paul's is described as "radical deviation."

8. See, for example, Roloff 1965:116-120, for a discussion of imitation entitled, "Vaterschaft und *mimêsis*," ("Fatherhood and Mimesis"). Roloff argues that the continuity of tradition is embodied in both of these notions—fatherhood and imitation—and that the two combine in Pauline discourse to incorporate the notions of teaching and imitation within the apostolic role. He collapses the distinction between imitation of Paul and imitation of Christ ("*Mimêsis tou Paulou ist mimêsis Christou!*") (Roloff 1965:119) and asserts that this equivalence actually reinscribes the authority of the apostle vis-à-vis the community, both as authority over, and mediating authority between Christ and the community (Roloff 1965:119-120). This paradoxical structure of, on the one hand, "imitation of Paul is imitation of Christ," and on the other hand, Paul's role as mediator, is a tension that is built into the mimetic relationship. Roloff does not resolve the tension or even remark upon it, but it is very much part of Pauline discourse of mimesis. It signals a level of confusion of identity, at least at the level of discourse, between Paul and Christ, a confusion that will be important for the later exegetical investigations of this study.

9. See especially Furnish 1968; Schnackenburg 1965; and others included in n. 1 to this chapter.

10. Two other works, those of Holmberg and Petersen, also attempt to address briefly the question of apostolic authority in relation to the language of imitation. In both cases, the authors accord the mimetic relationship a similar level of complexity to that which Schütz identifies, but there is a tension in both of their discourses as to

NOTES TO CHAPTER 2

whether the authoritative aspect of mimesis is really to be given full rhetorical weight. See, for example, Holmberg (1980:77-79) and Petersen (1985:130-131); also, see the discussion of these in the exegetical part of this inquiry, chapter four.

11. Fiore (1982:354-355) writes:

The Pauline homologoumena reflect the hortatory techniques and devices common to comparable writings of their day, some of which have been analyzed above. Example has been shown to be a prominent feature in Paul's hortatory method and he aims at imitation rather than obedience of his authoritative prescriptions. . . . At this point, one cannot fail to notice Paul's concern with the immediate occasion; the predominant position of his own example; and some formal differences in the way he employs example and other hortatory devices.

12. More specific points in Fiore's argument are taken up in the exegetical chapter of this work, chapter four.

NOTES TO CHAPTER 2
THEORETICAL FRAMEWORKS:
FOUCAULT AND POWER

1. See White 1978; Dreyfus and Rabinow 1982; Cousins and Hussain 1984; Deleuze 1988; Hoy 1986; Bernauer and Rasmussen 1988. On the impact of Foucault's thought on the human sciences, see especially Arac 1988; Diamond and Quinby 1988; Fraser 1989:17-66.

2. Foucault's concern with those who occupy the margins of a society made the "deviant" a favorite topic for him; the "deviant" is created and exists specifically so that the "norm" may be defined.

3. Nancy Fraser's use of the term "capillary" to describe Foucault's notion of power is a particularly felicitous image; see Fraser 1989:24 and elsewhere.

4. Megill 1985:248:

Foucault's 'analytic' of power turns out on close examination to be highly elusive. It seems to bear approximately the same relation to the exercise of power within the social order as Heidegger's reflections on 'technology' bear to actual technology. This amounts to saying that Foucault's 'analytic' ought to be read in ironic rather than in literalistic terms. It may certainly suggest to conventional historians, sociologists, and anthropologists ideas capable of animating their researches. But it is not itself worthy of our literal belief, for the whole question of its representational truth is not so much left in abeyance (this would be to underrate the imperiousness of the gesture) as ordered off the stage forever.

5. This point is crucial for a writer like Edward Said, who maintains a suspicion of the political usefulness of Foucault's analytics for contemporary struggles against domination. See Said 1986:153.

6. The complex relationships among economic, military, political, and ideological power within social networks are examined with insight and surprising breadth in Mann 1986. See especially Chapter 10, "Ideology Transcendent: the Christian *Ecumene*," 301-340.

7. Mann 1986:22-24. Foucault expresses the relationship between power and truth in terms of the relations between power and knowledge: see Foucault 1980d.

8. Discourse and its social effects are recurrent topics in Foucault's work, perhaps most clearly explicated in Foucault 1976.

9. Mann 1986:1: "*Societies are constituted of multiple overlapping and intersecting sociospatial networks of power. . . .* Societies are not unitary. They are not social systems (closed or open); they are not totalities."

10. Similarly, see Foucault 1976:1-15, where Foucault has demonstrated that "sexuality" is a nineteenth-century invention of discourse.

NOTES TO CHAPTER 3
THE FRAME OF REFERENCE:
DISCOURSES OF MIMESIS IN ANTIQUITY

1. Boisacq 1950:638-639; Frisk 1970:2:241; Chantraine 1968: 703-704. Both Frisk and Chantraine are dependent on two earlier works, Schulze 1966:53, which suggests a Sanskrit parallel (*mâyâ*) which means a "deceptive image" (Chantraine, "*image trompeuse*"; Frisk, "*Zauber(bild), Truggestalt, Betrug*"); and Schwyzer 1939:1:143, who claims merely that the term was borrowed from another language. Boisacq describes the etymology as "obscure," and offers the Sanskrit parallel of *mayatê* ("*troquer, échanger*") which he has taken from Prellwitz 1905:295.

2. Other early uses of the term *mimos* include Ar., *Thesm.* 17; Eur., *Rhes.* 256; Dem., *Ol.* 2.19. The Aristophanes reference is quite cryptic; Liddell-Scott-Jones reads the Euripides citation as "imitating or acting [a four-legged beast]," (Liddell and Scott 1925-40:1135); the Demosthenes text refers fairly obviously to actors. The early attesta-

tions of *mimeisthai* are somewhat more common; for a complete list, see Else 1958:73-90.

3. The imitation of God is discussed more fully in a later section (see pp. 83-93 below).

4. Havelock 1963:20-35; Sörbom 1966; Morrison 1982 (Part I: "Forming the Mimetic Tradition"):5-114; Tate 1928; Tate 1932; Greene 1918; McKeon 1936; Verdenius 1972; Russell and Winterbottom 1972; Atkins 1934; and, for Roman derivations of the Greek notion, see D'Alton 1931.

5. Pl., *Resp.* 597E: "This, then, [the characterization of the painter] will apply to the maker of tragedies also, if he is an imitator and is in his nature three removes from the king and the truth, as are all other imitators?"

6. Pl., *Resp.* 598E-599D:

For the good poet, if he is to poetize things rightly, must, they [critics] argue, create with knowledge or else be unable to create. So we must consider whether these critics have not fallen in with such imitators and been deceived by them, so that looking upon their works they cannot perceive that these are three removes from reality, and easy to produce without knowledge of the truth. For it is phantoms, not realities that they produce . . . . Do you suppose, then, that if a man were able to produce both the exemplar and the semblance, he would be eager to abandon himself to the fashioning of phantoms and set this in the forefront of his life as the best thing he had? . . . if he had genuine knowledge of the things he imitates he would far rather devote himself to real things than to the imitation of them, and would endeavour to leave after him many noble deeds and works as memorials of himself, and would be eager to be the theme of praise than the praiser.

7. See, for example, Pl., *Resp.* 602A-B, 603A-605C; *Soph.* 241E, 264D, 265A, 267B, 268C-D; *Plt.* 299C-E, 303C; *Ep.* 5, 321E.

8. The Platonic text's ironic relationship to mimesis was first suggested to me by a paper read by Professor Aryeh Kosman of Haverford College, "Silence and Imitation in Plato," 9 April 1986, at Pitzer College, Claremont, CA. As far as I know, this paper has not been published.

9. Diels Kranz 68 B 34. For a similar notion, see Hippoc., *Vict.* I,21 (Diels Kranz 22 C 1), where the human being is described as a

microcosm in all aspects and activities: its nature, activity, speech, writing, and art.

10. This notion has been discussed extensively in the literature. For a summary, see Burkert 1972:43-45.

11. For a general commentary on this text, see Cornford 1937; also see Rutenber 1946 (chapter 4, "The Unconscious Imitation of God"):40-57.

12. See Pl., *Ti.* 28A-B, where the visible, tangible, corporeal—and therefore, sensible—characteristics are assigned to creatures.

13. This point is expressed later in *Ti.* (69B-D) where the emphasis is on the unity and orderliness of the universe:

> As we stated at the commencement, all these things were in a state of disorder, when God implanted in them proportions both severally in relation to themselves and in their relations to one another, so far as it was in any way possible for them to be in harmony and proportion. For at that time nothing partook thereof, save by accident, nor was it possible to name anything worth mentioning which bore the names we now give them . . . ; but He, in the first place, set all these in order, and then out of these He constructed this present Universe, one single Living Creature containing within itself all living creatures both mortal and immortal. And He Himself acts as the Constructor of things divine, but the structure of the mortal things He commanded His own engendered sons to execute. And they, imitating him (*hoi de mimoumenoi*), on receiving the immortal principle of soul, framed around it a mortal body, and gave it all the body to be its vehicle, and housed therein besides another form of soul . . . .

14. The verb "to follow" here is *hepesthai*, which is also a technical term for a kind of imitation of the divine. Cf. the Pythagorean precept articulated by Aristoxenus, that *to akolouthein tô theô* is the keynote of the Pythagorean system (Burnet 1919:526a), and the anonymous excerpt in Stob., *Ecl.* 2.249.8, which gives *hepou theô* ("follow God") as a Pythagorean precept, and connects it with Pl., *Tht.* 176B-D. Also, one might take note of the technical significance of *akolouthein* in the synoptic traditions about Jesus (Betz 1967:5-47).

15. There are many examples from Philo which would sustain this comparison. See for example, *Aet. Mund.* 15; *Virt.* 12; *Spec. 'Leg.* 1. 14, 83ff.; 2. 2, 141, 151, 224-225; *Decal.* 51; *Vit. Mos.* II, 11, 117, 127, 128, 133, 135, 153; *Rer. Div. Her.* 165; *Migr. Abr.* 40; *Leg. All.*

I, 43, 45; *Op. Mund.* 25, 133 (where he invokes Pl., *Menex.* 238A), 139; *Ebr.* 133.

16. Vogel 1966:183 suggests that this may not be the form in which Pythagoras's doctrine was stated, but this was certainly his sentiment.

17. Vogel (1966:71-74, 184) draws the connection between this Platonic text and Pythagorean ideology of following God. In addition, he cites the same sequence: gods—demons—heroes—parents elsewhere in Iambl., *VP* 100, 144, 175; D.L. 8.23 (on Pythagoras); Porph., *Plot.* 38; Pl., *Resp.* 392A, 427B.

18. Rutenber (1946:38-39) stresses this point: the gap between humanity and God which can never be bridged. Further, Rutenber argues that all the references to likeness to God (whether cosmologically or anthropologically) emphasize the limits of the possible achievement of this ideal. He cites *Ti.* 29E; *Resp.* 500C f., 501B, 613A; *Phdr.* 249C; *Tht.* 176B; *Leg.* 716C.

19. Frischer 1982:124-125: "We know that Epicurean groups were organized hierarchically according to very precise *scalae sapientiae*. Just as the sage perfected himself by imitating the gods, his students perfected themselves by imitating him, and they advanced up successive rungs of the ladder as they did so."

20. An important distinction, also, lies in the fact of Epicurean anthropomorphosis of the gods; see Frischer 1982:78-79 and n. 39.

21. Merki 1952:8: "The idea of *akolouthôs tê phusei zên* was also later designated as a goal for human beings. In the equality of nature and God arose the equality between 'following nature' and 'following God'" (translation mine). Here he cites as evidence Epict., *Diss.* 1.12.5 ("For if gods do not exist, how can it be an end to follow the gods [*pôs esti telos hepesthai theois*]?") and 1.30.4 ("When you come into the presence of some prominent man, remember that Another [i.e., God] looks from above on what is taking place, and that you must please Him rather than this man. He, then, who is above asks of you, . . . 'And what was the "end"?' 'To follow Thee [*to soi akolouthein*].'") Merki concludes, "In the middle and late Stoa the motif of *homoiôsis theô* [being like God] also came to have value and ran parallel to the formula enumerated earlier [following God], without itself being designated as a goal" (my translation).

22. Malherbe 1977:194 (Heraclitus, *Epistle* 5, To Amphidamas, ll. 6-12). See also Malherbe 1977:198 (Heraclitus, *Epistle* 6, To Amphidamas, ll. 19-20).

23. *Letter of Aristeas* 188 ("You would administer [the kingdom] best by imitating the eternal goodness of God," Charlesworth 1983-85:2:25); 210 ("For, as God does good to the whole world, so you by imitating him would be without offense," Charlesworth 1983-85:2:26); 280 ("Men who hate wickedness, and in imitation of his way of life do justice," Charlesworth 1983-85:2:31); 281 ("As God showers blessings upon all, you too in imitation of him are a benefactor to your subjects," Charlesworth 1983-85:2:31).

24. See also *Decal.* 51 ("Thus one set of enactments begins with God the Father and Maker of all, and ends with parents who copy His nature [*hoi mimoumenoi tên ekeinou physin*] by begetting particular persons"); *Decal.* 111 ("those who brought them forth from non-existence to existence and in this were imitators of God [*mimêsamenous theon*]"); *Spec. Leg.* 2.2 ("For parents are copies and like-nesses of the divine power [*apeikonismata gar houtoi ge kai mimêmata theias dunameôs eisi*], since they have brought the non-existence into existence"); *Spec. Leg.* 2.224-225 ("For parents are midway between the natures of God and man, and partake of both; the human obviously because they have been born and will perish, the divine because they have brought others to the birth and have raised not-being into being. Parents, in my opinion, are to their children what God is to the world, since just as He achieved existence for the non-existent, so they in imitation [*mimoumenoi*] of His power, as far as they are capable, immortalize the race").

25. The essential text for considering the question of hellenistic kingship continues to be Goodenough 1928. For an excellent general survey of ancient political philosophy through the Byzantine period, see Dvornik 1966.

26. See also Isoc., *Ep. ad Phil.* II:5, where the idea of becoming a god (*genesthai theon*) is invoked.

27. An example of the idea of the innate quality of the king's power may be found in the fragments of Ecphantus the Pythagorean in Stob., *Ecl.* 4.7.64-66 (see Dvornik 1966:254): "Thus royalty is explained with the fact that by its divine character and excessive brilliance it is hard to behold, except for those who have a legitimate claim. For bastard usurpers are confuted by complete bedazzlement and by such vertigo as assails those who climb to a lofty height. But royalty is, then, a sure and incorruptible thing, very hard for a human being to achieve by reason of its exceeding divinity . . . . And the one who lives in royalty ought to share in its immaculate nature and to understand how much more divine than he are those others [the

gods], to whom, by likening himself, he would do the best for himself and his subjects."

28. Stob., *Ecl.* 4.7.65 (Goodenough 1928:89). Similar articulations of the same point may be found in the Letter to Alexander which introduces the [*Rh. Al.*] (1420B) and Plu., *Ad Principem ineruditum, Mor.* 779-782 (see Dvornik 1966:259-260, 270-273; Goodenough 1928:92, 96).

29. Dvornik 1966:252-253 says the fragment is not genuine, but dates it to the second century BCE.

30. Musonius Rufus, fragment on kingship: "And generally it is absolutely necessary for the good king to be faultless in his arguments and in his acts and perfect, if he would be as the men of old thought a law animate pursuing a good system of laws and harmony and repelling lawlessness and sedition, being an imitator of Zeus and like him a father of his subjects" (Dvornik 1966:536). Cf. also Dio Chrys., *Or.* I, 12; 37; 40.

31. See Koller 1954:58-9 for a demonstration of the connections between *mimêsis* and *mathêsis*.

32. Later in the same work, Xenophon narrates Antipho's chastisement of Socrates for his poor example: "Now the professors of other subjects try to make their pupils copy (*mimêtas*) their teachers: if you too intend to make your companions do that, you must consider yourself a professor of unhappiness" (*Mem.* 1.6.3).

33. The literature on rhetorical education and the role of imitation within it is quite extensive. The fundamental surveys continue to be the works of Kennedy 1963; 1972; 1980. A less helpful, basic treatment of the subject may be found Clark 1951; 1957, esp. chapter 5, 144-176. For the role of imitation in rhetorical theory of the Roman period, two articles are particularly useful: Fantham 1978a; 1978b. See also Price 1975.

34. Dion. Hal. (see Usener and Radermacher ed. 1904-1929:2: 197-217). The subject matter of the three fragmentary books on imitation is described by Dionysius in his *Pomp.* 3, where he writes:

> The first of these contains an abstract inquiry into the nature of imitation. The second asks what particular poets and philosophers, historians and orators, should be imitated. The third, which treats of the proper manner of imitation, remains unfinished (1901:105).

35. Kennedy 1972:383:

> Although we cannot claim that this imitation is a deliberate counterpart of the imitation taught by classicizing rhetoricians

such as the Neo-Atticists, a similar philosophy lies behind the technique: excellence can be imparted to the contemporary by a careful study of the noble quality of the past. . . . [T]he new Augustan 'rhetoric' inculcated a moral imitation of the creed of the heroes of the past, especially the half-legendary heroes of earlier Rome. The goal was a style of life: patriotic, serious, self-sacrificing. The poetry of Horace and Vergil and the history of Livy set forth these models in the grandest terms, and Augustus lost no opportunity to present them visually to the Romans.

36. Democr. Fr. 39 (Diels Kranz 2:155.5): "It is necessary either to be good or to imitate the good." Democr. Fr. 79 (Diels Kranz 2:160.5f.): "It is a grievous thing to imitate evil men, and not even wish to imitate good ones."

37. See, for example, Philo, *Vit. Mos.* 1.158-159:

Again, was not the joy of his partnership with the Father and Maker of all magnified also by the honor of being deemed worthy to bear the same title? For he was named god and king of the whole nation, and entered, we are told, into the darkness where God was, that is into the unseen, invisible, incorporeal and archetypal essence of existing things. Thus he beheld what is hidden from the sight of mortal nature, and, in himself, his life displayed for all to see, he has set before us, like some well-wrought picture, a piece of work beautiful and godlike, a model for those who are willing to copy it. Happy are they who imprint, or strive to imprint, that image in their souls. For it were best that the mind should carry the form of virtue in perfection, but, failing this, let it at least have the unflinching desire to possess that form.

Note the influence of Platonic theory of forms in this description of the relationship of Moses to God, and also the derivative nature of the mimetic relationship as expressed in the last sentence. On the idea of the imitation of Moses generally, see Mack 1972. Other relevant texts from Philo include *Virt.* 66; *Praem. Poen.* 115; *Spec. Leg.* 2.141; 4.55; 4.173; 4.182; 4.188; *Abr.* 38; *Vit. Mos.* 1.303. References to negative ethical imitation appear frequently in Philo; see *Leg. Gai.* 87-88; *Vit. Cont.* 62; *Spec. Leg.* 3.125; *Vit. Mos.* 2.162, 2.270.

38. For example, *Ant.* 6.342; 6.347; 8.24; 8.193; 8.196; 8.251-252; 8.300; 8.315; 9.44; 9.99; 9.173; 9.243; 9.282; 10.37; 10.47; 10.50; 12.203; 12.241; 13.5; 17.97; 17.109-110; 17.245-246; 18.291. Also see *Ap.* 2.204 and 2.270.

39. Karl Frederick Morrison, in *The Mimetic Tradition of Reform in the West* (1982), argues that mimesis has always functioned as a mediator between asymmetries, a way of reconciling difference (xiii-xiv). Furthermore, he understands its goal in Greco-Roman antiquity to be unity, worked out as a corrective strategy (17 and elsewhere). While Morrison demonstrates this aspect of mimesis—the drive toward sameness and unity—he ignores the political aspect of this drive. That is, the mimetic system which Morrison identifies as a dominant force in the formation and transformation of Western culture and its self-reflection, presupposes that "wholeness," nondifferentiation, is a positive value. In short, the system operates under the assumption that sameness represents harmony and difference represents discord. Imitation is essential to the establishment and sustenance of unity, harmony, and sameness. The preceding overview of the discursive applications of mimesis in Greco-Roman antiquity should have demonstrated this point very clearly. Morrison's argument suggests that the processes at work in what he calls the "mimetic tradition of reform" are at the heart of the Western tradition, providing a crucial part of the foundation of Western culture.

NOTES TO CHAPTER 4
"BE IMITATORS OF ME":
DISCOURSES OF MIMESIS IN PAUL

1. Michaelis 1967:670: "The co-ordination of Paul and the Lord here does not prevent us from seeing in *kai tou kyriou* an intensifying, whether it be by way of self-correction (cf. 1 C. 15:10), or whether it be that the recognition afforded the community is to be deepened and extended." De Boer 1962:121 argues specifically against the notion of the construction evoking a self-correction on the basis of the fact that Paul makes no such attempt in the other passages where he exhorts the early communities to become his imitators; he cites 1 Cor 4:16, Phil 3:17, and includes 2 Thess 3:7-9 as a Pauline text.

2. See Dick 1900:4-14 and Rigaux 1950:77-79, esp. 77 n. 6, for summaries of the scholarly discussion of the use of the first-person plural in Paul's letters in general and in the Thessalonian correspondence in particular.

3. Rigaux characterizes the nature of the first-person plural in this context as producing the sense of a united and univocal apostolic witness:

> The first persons of our letters are governed by a very particular intention. Paul retreats from the apostolic group in order

to stress their wills or personal actions . . . . The meaning of
'we' is more subtle. There isn't a lone plural that could be
true. In these cases where one could doubt it, inasmuch as the
tone is individual and the style belonging to Paul, one will
read only a clearer accent on the apostolic will, which pres-
ents the Christian message as the work of the entire group.
The common function, work, and preaching take primacy over
the individual. Completely true to the gospel, Paul prefers to
disappear in the group. This is why, when he sends a letter,
he includes those who work with him . . . . One could think in
the plural of the apostolate and the witness. (Rigaux 1950:79)

4. For a general discussion of the uses of the indicative and the
imperative in Paul, see Betz 1967:169-186.

5. Pearson 1971 has been particularly influential in putting forward the argument that the text is a later interpolation. More recently,
John C. Hurd has argued, from the perspective of methodological
considerations and from the structure of the letter itself, that the
passage must be retained as Pauline (Hurd 1986:172).

6. Patte 133 argues that the Thessalonians are *mimêtai* not because "they follow their [the Judean churches'] example, but [be-
cause] the same things *happened* to them."

7. LSJ, s.v. *sun*, 1690-1691: "D. IN COMPOS. I. *with, along with,
at the same time*, hence any kind of union, connexion, or participation
in a thing, and metaph. of agreement or unity." See also McGrath
1952; Grundmann 1971.

De Boer 1962:177-179 summarizes the various scholarly conclusions on the nature of the *sun*-prefix in this context, and he also
concludes that the sense of it has to do with a call to unity:

Basically it was a subtle call to unity. Such a call applied to
all. It was important that everyone do his part in promoting
unity of effort and action. However, for the deviating ones it
was a special call to join with the more faithful ones in their
imitation. At the same time the more faithful brethren were
called by it to be helpful in regard to the deviating ones. They
must so live and act as to encourage a more consistent and
total imitation from those who were taking too many liberties
in doctrine and life" (de Boer 1962:179).

8. Betz 1967:162ff makes this observation and notes in connection with it that the mimesis which is being called for is distinct from
any notion of following the earthly Jesus; rather, he argues, this

connection with the Christ hymn in Philippians makes it clear that a form of *imitatio Christi* is being demanded. See also Betz 1967:186.

9. This claim about the structure of the rhetoric here is justified on the basis of the repetition which Betz 1967:154 has noted, connecting these two passages philologically: *parakalô de humas* in 1:10 is echoed in the *parakalô oun humas* in 4:16.

10. For a detailed treatment of the image of Paul as father, see Gutierrez 1968. On the relationship between this spiritual paternity and the idea of imitation, see pp. 178-188.

11. See the discussion of the *paterfamilias* and *patria potestas* Crook 1967:107-113; Nicholas 1962:65-68, 76-80.

12. Petersen 1985:130-31:

From these texts [cited in a previous paragraph] it is evident not only that the notion of 'father' metaphorically describes Paul's apostolic role, and that the generation of his metaphorical children is through the 'seed' of the gospel he preached, but it is also evident that the parent-child metaphoric complex expresses a hierarchical social structural relationship. Indeed, it is a form of Paul's social relations that explicitly expresses his social structural relationship with the churches . . . . Although the metaphor of 'father' is one of ambiguous superiority, Paul expressly prefers to admonish rather than to shame, to be gentle rather than firm, to give of himself rather than take from his children . . . . Throughout, love is the familial or kinship quality that expressly motivates his behavior, but for Paul, love can also be expressed in shaming, just as edification can be expressed in tearing down.

13. Bauer 1979:513 says that the use of the term here is unique. Generally, it means "change the form of, transform, change" or "say something with the aid of a figure of speech." The lexicon gives the sense of the use here as "I have given this teaching of mine the form of an exposition concerning Apollos and myself;" also Schneider 1971. Allo 1934:71 characterizes the term *metaschêmatizô* as "one of the embarrassing words of the Pauline vocabulary" (my translation). De Boer 1962:141 summarizes the medieval and reformation interpretations, and interprets the passage as meaning "that what he has written is a veiled allusion from which they must learn," and that Paul has used himself and Apollos as examples to avoid naming the names of the guilty in Corinth. Conzelmann 1975:85-86 summarizes the modern possibilities, and states, "Here it must be conceded that this use of *metaschêmatizein* ('exemplify') is catachrestic." He also cites, at 86 n.

10, Hooker 1963/4:127-132, who identifies the figurative reference as the recurring metaphors of planting and building. Fiore 1982:321-322, in contrast to these other interpreters, argues that, because the section has to do both with factionalism and with the question of special knowledge or wisdom, that the analogical interpretation of *metaschêmatizein* is insufficient and that Apollos and Paul in effect become themselves rhetorical figures.

14. A summary of the various interpretations may be found in Wallis 1950. Weiss 1925:103 proposes that it is parallel with *hina mê*, and notes the suggestion that it might well reflect a marginal gloss that worked its way into the manuscript tradition. Moffatt 1938:46 says "the meaning lies beyond recovery." Conzelmann 1975:86 characterizes the phrase as "unintelligible," and calls any other interpretative attempt "guesswork." De Boer 1962:142-143 summarizes the various possibilities and ultimately states that the problem of interpretation is unresolvable: "Paul shows by what he proceeds immediately to say that his real intent in the passage is not to speak on the normativity of Scripture, but to strike at the haughtiness, the pride, the egotistic self-sufficiency, and the consequent contentiousness of the Corinthians. We leave the exact meaning of the phrase 'not to go beyond the things which are written' in abeyance, observing simply that it somehow helped to make this latter point."

15. Bauer 1979:593 takes *oun* to be primarily inferential, "denoting that what it introduces is the result of or an inference from what precedes *so, therefore, consequently, accordingly, then.*"

16. Fiore 1982:324-325 offers this explanation for the tension:

> The problem of factionalism is an outgrowth of the faulty wisdom and judgment in the community. The negation of factionalism rests on a positive growth in wisdom and judgment (1:10; 3:1-4; 3:18; 4:5). The common apostolic model, while applied to wisdom (1:18-25; 2:6-16) and judgment (2:13-15), is more apt for undercutting the factional lionizing of one teacher over another by depicting their harmonious cooperation with the particularized gifts from God (3:5-15). The fundamental qualities of wisdom and judgment are taken by Paul as his special responsibility, since he alone laid the foundations of the community's faith (2:1-5; 3:10-11). The intrusion of Paul's example in these first chapters leads to its exclusive application in the rest of the letter, as the fundamental issue of the community's wisdom and judgment is faced in a variety of settings. *Mimêsis* and *metaschêmatisis* merge, and the virtuous example that Paul urges the community to imitate

emerges as his own. Paul's life and teaching become a metaphor for the community's striving, as they seek to become like their founder and father.

17. D. Williams 1967:341 shares this position, but also throughout his work tends to collapse the ideas of teaching and imitation; his thesis is that Paul teaches through his own personal example.

18. See, for example, Foucault's description of the functioning of the technology of power, the Panopticon, in *Discipline and Punish* (Foucault 1979:195-218). I thank Michael Humphries for pointing out this connection to me.

19. This occurs also in Rom 2:16.

20. De Boer 1962:150-151 tries to smooth over this rhetorical difficulty by claiming that Paul really means "in a Christian way," "the Christian life as he now lives it wherever he goes."

21. De Boer (1962) refers to "*kathôs kagô Christou*" as a final stroke of the pen" (161) and a "parting flourish" (164), discounting any significance at all of the mention of Paul's imitation of Christ and arguing that any interpretation which tries to see *imitatio Christi* in this passage is anachronistically influenced by later spiritual reflection (161). Likewise, the debate between Michaelis (1967) and Stanley (1959) breaks down along Protestant-Catholic lines. See also D. Williams 1967:353.

22. Robertson and Plummer 1914:225 attempt to explain this relation as a way for Paul to avoid the arrogance of his call to imitation. D. Williams 1967:352 n. 158, in response, says that such a position only "shows how far removed they are from the teaching presuppositions of the first century."

23. De Boer 1962:188-196; Stanley 1959:874-876; Bonnard 1953:91; Schlier 1949:147; Lagrange 1925:109; Betz 1979:221-223. Notably, Michaelis 1967:675 n. 29 states categorically that this text is not related to the Pauline discourse of mimesis, and cites as his authority Oepke 1937:104-105.

NOTES TO CHAPTER 5
READING EFFECTS:
IMITATION, POWER, AND CLAIMS TO TRUTH

1. "Sliding signification" describes the process by which language is related to its referents. Rather than seeing language as a simple, transparent linguistic overlay of "reality," the notion of "sliding signification" suggests that language is not fixed on to reality in a

simple fashion, but moves in relation to it, slides over its referents, resulting in meanings that are often multiple, displaced, unintentional.

2. It is quite striking, however, how relatively quickly those institutional moves are made in the formation of the church, and further how they are made by writers who are explicit imitators of Paul—the authors of the pastoral epistles.

3. For one of the clearest introductions to Derrida's thought and its implications for cultural criticism, see Culler 1982; see also Megill 1985:257-337.

4. The field is wide-ranging here, not easily summarized. See, among other important works, Trinh 1988 and 1989; Mudimbe 1988; *Inscriptions*; and the writings of cultural workers such as Gayatri Chakravorty Spivak, Edward Said, Chandra Talpade Mohanty, among others.

5. These issues are discussed widely in writings by post-colonial and some feminist theorists; one particularly helpful exposition of the layerings of difficulties around these questions may be found in Trinh 1989:79-118.

6. The full history of the effects of missionary discourse on indigenous cultures has yet to be written, though there have been significant meaningful starts made on such a project. Mudimbe 1988:44-97 offers some direction for future work in this area.

7. The setting aside of particular interests has long been deemed unacceptable by those struggling to bring about cultural and social change. The example of Martin Luther King Jr.'s arguments in "The Letter from Birmingham Jail" is a modern case-in-point in contemporary American political struggle over sameness and difference in relation to racial identities (see especially King 1964:80-81). I thank Francis Miller, whose work on King's writings brought this example to mind for me, and who located the particular citation for me.

8. I must thank Hal Taussig for the notion of "over-extension," which he has used in a rather different context in personal conversation, but which resonates helpfully here.

9. I owe thanks to Christina Crosby for this very useful term, "duopoly." Personal conversation, December 1990.

10. See J. Scott 1988 and Riley 1988 for analyses of the discursive limits of nineteenth- and twentieth-century English and American feminisms around the problematic of sameness and difference.

11. In personal conversation, November 1990.

BIBLIOGRAPHY

TEXTS AND TRANSLATIONS

[Within the text, ancient sources are abbreviated according to the standard set by *The Oxford Classical Dictionary*. The editions included in this bibliography are those consulted; translations are mine when no translation is cited in the bibliography.]

Aelian. 1971. *Claudii Aeliani de natura animalium libri xvii, varia historia, epistolae, fragmenta*. 2 vols. Repr. ed. Graz: Akademische Druck- und Verlagsanstalt.

Aeschylus. 1963. *Aeschylus*. 2 vols. Trans. Herbert Weir Smyth. LCL. Cambridge: Harvard Univ.

Aristophanes. 1927-30. *Aristophanes*. 3 vols. Trans. Benjamin Bickley Rogers. LCL. Cambridge: Harvard Univ.

Aristotle. 1927. *The "Art" of Rhetoric*. Trans. John H. Freese. LCL. Cambridge: Harvard Univ.

—— 1936a. *Metaphysics*. 2 vols. Trans. H. Tredennick. LCL. Cambridge: Harvard Univ.

—— 1936b. *Problems and Rhetorica ad Alexandrum*. 2 vols. Trans. H. Rackham and W. S. Hett. LCL. Cambridge: Harvard Univ.

—— 1939. *Poetics and Longinus*. Trans. W. Hamilton Frye. LCL. Cambridge: Harvard Univ.

—— 1950. *Politics*. Trans. H. Rackham. LCL. Cambridge: Harvard Univ.

—— 1984. *The Complete Works*. The Revised Oxford Translation. 2 vols. Bollingen Series 121. Ed. Jonathan Barnes. Princeton: Princeton Univ.

Arnim, Ioannes von, ed. 1986. *Stoicorum Veterum Fragmenta*. Repr. ed. 4 vols. New York: Irvington.

Cicero. 1966. *Pro Caecina, Pro Lege Manilia, Pro Cluentio, Pro Rabirio*. Trans. H. Grose Hodge. LCL. Cambridge: Harvard Univ.

—— 1971. *Tusculan Disputations*. Trans. J. E. King. LCL. Cambridge: Harvard Univ.

Demosthenes. 1930. *Olynthiacs, Philippics, Minor Orations I-XVII, XX*. Trans. J. H. Vince. LCL. Cambridge: Harvard Univ.

Diels, Hermann, and Wilhelm Kranz, eds. 1951-52. *Die Fragmente der Vorsokratiker*. 3 vols. 6th ed. Zürich: Weidmann.

Dio Chrysostom. 1932. *Discourses*. 5 vols. Trans. James W. Cohoon and H. Lamar Crosby. LCL. Cambridge: Harvard Univ.

Diogenes Laertius. 1925. *Lives of Eminent Philosophers*. 2 vols. Trans. Robert D. Hicks. LCL. Cambridge: Harvard Univ.

Dionysius of Halicarnassus. 1901. *The Three Literary Letters*. Ed. and trans. W. Rhys Roberts. Cambridge: Cambridge Univ.

—— 1904-29. *Dionysii Halicarnasei quae exstant*. 6 vols. Ed. Hermann Usener and Ludwig Radermacher. Leipzig: Teubner.

Epictetus. 1926. *The Discourses as Reported by Arrian, the Manual, and Fragments*. Trans. William A. Oldfather. LCL. Cambridge: Harvard Univ.

Euripides. 1912. *Euripides*. 4 vols. Trans. A. S. Way. LCL. Cambridge: Harvard Univ.

Hermogenes. 1913. *Opera*. Ed. Hugo Rabe. Leipzig: Teubner.

Iamblichus. 1965. *De Vita Pythagorica*. Ed. Augustus Nauck. Repr. ed. Amsterdam: Hakkert.

Isocrates. 1928. *Isocrates*. 3 vols. Trans. George Norlin. LCL. Cambridge: Harvard Univ.

Josephus. 1976. *The Life, Against Apion*. Trans. H. St. J. Thackeray. LCL. Cambridge: Harvard Univ.

—— 1978-81. *Jewish Antiquities*. 7 vols. Trans. H. St. J. Thackeray, Ralph Marcus, Allen Wikgren, and L. H. Feldman. LCL. Cambridge: Harvard Univ.

[Longinus]. 1964. *On the Sublime*. Ed. D. A. Russell. Oxford: Clarendon.

Malherbe, Abraham J., comp. and ed. 1977. *The Cynic Epistles: A Study Edition*. Missoula: Scholars.

Nauck, Augustus, ed. 1964 . *Tragicorum Graecorum fragmenta*. 2d ed. Leipzig: Teubner, 1889; repr. with *Supplementum*, ed. B. Snell. Hildeheim: Olms.

Philo. 1929. *Philo*. 12 vols. Trans. Francis H. Colson and George H. Whitaker. LCL. Cambridge: Harvard Univ.

Plato. 1914. *Euthyphro, Apology, Crito, Phaedo, Phaedrus*. Trans. Harold N. Fowler. LCL. Cambridge: Harvard Univ.

—— 1924. *Laches, Protagoras, Meno, Euthydemus*. Trans. C. W. Lamb. LCL. Cambridge: Harvard Univ.

—— 1925. *Lysias, Symposium, Gorgias*. Trans. C. W. Lamb. LCL. Cambridge: Harvard Univ.

—— 1926. *Laws*. 2 vols. Trans. R. G. Bury. LCL. Cambridge: Harvard Univ.

—— 1929. *Timaeus, Critias, Cleitophon, Menexenus, Epistles*. Trans. R. G. Bury. LCL. Cambridge: Harvard Univ.

—— 1930-35. *Republic*. 2 vols. Trans. Paul Shorey. LCL. Cambridge: Harvard Univ.

Plato (cont.). 1961. *The Collected Dialogues, including the Letters.* Ed. Edith Hamilton and Huntington Cairns. Bollingen Series 71. Princeton: Princeton Univ.

—— 1975. *Statesman, Philebus, Ion.* Trans. Harold N. Fowler and W. R. M. Lamb. LCL. Cambridge: Harvard Univ.

—— 1977. *Theaetetus, Sophist.* Trans. Harold N. Fowler. LCL. Cambridge: Harvard Univ.

Plutarch. 1969. *Moralia.* 15 vols. Trans. Frank C. Babbitt and Harold N. Fowler. LCL. Cambridge: Harvard Univ.

Porphyry. 1963. *Vita Pythagorae* in *Porphyrii philosophi Platonici opuscula selecta.* 2d ed. Repr. ed. Ed. Augustus Nauck. Hildesheim: Olms.

Quintilian. 1920. *Institutio Oratoria.* 4 vols. Trans. Harold E. Butler. LCL. Cambridge: Harvard Univ.

Seneca. 1928. *Moral Essays.* 3 vols. Trans. John W. Basore. LCL. Cambridge: Harvard Univ.

Stobaeus. 1958. *Anthologium.* 2 vols. Ed. Curtius Wachsmuth and Otto Hense. Berlin: Weidmann.

Xenophon. 1979. *Memorabilia, Oeconomicus, Symposium, Apology.* Trans. E. C. Marchant and O. J. Todd. LCL. Cambridge: Harvard Univ.

MODERN SOURCES

[Abbreviations for periodical and other standard literature in the field follow the standard set by the *Journal of Biblical Literature.*]

Abrahams, J. 1924. "The Imitation of God." In *Studies in Pharisaism and the Gospels.* 2d ser. Cambridge: Cambridge Univ. Pp. 138-192.

Adrados, Francisco R. 1975. *Festival, Comedy, and Tragedy: The Greek Origins of Theatre.* Trans. Christopher Holme. Leiden: Brill.

Aerts, Th. 1966. "Suivre Jesus. Evolution d'un thème biblique dans les Evangiles Synoptiques." *ETL* 42:476-512.

Agacinski, Sylviane, Jacques Derrida, Sarah Kofman, Philippe Lacoue-Labarthe, Jean-Luc Nancy, Renard Pautrat. 1975. *Mimesis des articulations.* Paris: Flammarion.

Allmen, Daniel von. 1981. *La famille de Dieu. La symbolique familiale dans le Paulinisme.* Orbis Biblicus et Orientalis 41. Göttingen: Vandenhoeck & Ruprecht.

Allo, E.-B. 1934. *St Paul: Première épître aux Corinthiens.* Études Bibliques. Paris: Gabalda.

Arac, Jonathan, ed. 1988. *After Foucault: Humanistic Knowledge, Postmodern Challenges.* New Brunswick, NJ: Rutgers Univ.

Atkins, J. W. H. 1934. *Literary Criticism in Antiquity: A Sketch of its Development*. 2 vols. Cambridge: Cambridge Univ.

Auerbach, Erich. 1953. *Mimesis: The Representation of Reality in Western Literature*. Trans. Willard R. Trask. Princeton: Princeton Univ.

Bauer, Walter. 1934. *Rechtgläubigkeit und Ketzerei im ältesten Christentum*. Beiträge zur historischen Theologie 10. Tübingen: Mohr (Siebeck). ET: *Orthodoxy and Heresy in Earliest Christianity*. Ed. Robert Kraft and Gerhard Krodel. Trans. Philadelphia Seminar on Christian Origins. Philadelphia: Fortress, 1971.

—— 1979. *A Greek-English Lexicon of the New Testament and Other Early Christian Literature*. 2d rev. ed. from the 5th German ed. F. Wilbur Gingrich and Frederick W. Danker. Chicago: Univ. of Chicago.

Bernauer, James, and Thomas Keenan. 1988. "The Works of Michel Foucault, 1954-1984." In Bernauer and Rasmussen 1988:119-158.

Bernauer, James, and David Rasmussen, eds. 1988. *The Final Foucault*. Cambridge: MIT.

Best, Ernest. 1955. *One Body in Christ: A Study in the Relationship of the Church to Christ in the Epistles of the Apostle Paul*. London: SPCK.

Betz, Hans Dieter. 1967. *Nachfolge und Nachahmung Jesu Christi im Neuen Testament*. Beiträge zur historischen Theologie 37. Tübingen: Mohr (Siebeck).

—— 1979. *Galatians: A Commentary*. Hermeneia. Philadelphia: Fortress.

Blumenthal, Albrecht von. 1928. "ΤΥΠΟΣ und ΠΑΡΑΔΕΙΓΜΑ." *Hermes* 63:391-414.

Boer, Willis Peter de. 1962. *The Imitation of Paul: An Exegetical Study*. Kampen: Kok.

Boisacq, Emile. 1950. *Dictionnaire étymologique de la langue grecque*. 4th ed. Heidelberg: Winter.

Bonnard, Pierre. 1953. *L'Épître de saint Paul aux Galates*. CNT 9. Neuchâtel: Delachaux et Niestlé.

Bourdieu, Pierre. 1977. *Outline of a Theory of Practice*. Trans. Richard Nick. Cambridge Studies in Social Anthropology 16. New York: Cambridge Univ.

Buber, Martin. 1926. "Nachahmung Gottes." *Morgen* 1:638-647.

Bultmann, Rudolf. 1933. *Glauben und Verstehen*, Vol. 1. Tübingen: Mohr (Siebeck).

Burkert, Walter. 1972. *Lore and Science in Ancient Pythagoreanism*. Trans. Edwin L. Minar, Jr. Cambridge: Harvard Univ.

Burnet, J. 1919. "Pythagoras and Pythagoreanism." *Encyclopedia of Religion and Ethics* 10:520-530.

Campenhausen, Hans F. von, Kurt Galling, et al., eds. 1950ff. *Die Religion in Geschichte und Gegenwart: Handwörterbuch für Theologie und Religionswissenschaft.* 3d rev. ed. Tübingen: Mohr (Siebeck).

Cerfaux, Lucien. 1954. *Le Christ dans la théologie de Saint Paul.* 2d rev. ed. Lectio Divina 6. Paris: Cerf.

—— 1962. *Le Chrétien dans la théologie paulinienne.* Lectio Divina 33. Paris: Cerf.

Chantraine, Pierre. 1968. *Dictionnaire étymologique de la langue grecque.* Paris: Klincksieck.

Charlesworth, James H., ed. 1983-85. *The Old Testament Pseudepigrapha.* 2 vols. Garden City, NY: Doubleday.

Clark, Donald Lemen. 1951. "Imitation: Theory and Practice in Roman Rhetoric." *Quarterly Journal of Speech* 37:11-22.

—— 1957. *Rhetoric in Greco-Roman Education.* Morningside Heights, NY: Columbia Univ.

Conzelmann, Hans. 1975. *1 Corinthians: A Commentary.* Trans. James Leitch. Hermeneia. Philadelphia: Fortress.

Cornford, Francis MacDonald. 1922/23. "Mysticism and Science in the Pythagorean Tradition." *CQ* 16:137-150; 17:1-12.

—— 1937. *Plato's Cosmology: The Timaeus of Plato Translated with a Running Commentary.* New York: Harcourt, Brace.

Cousins, Mark and Athar Hussain. 1984. *Michel Foucault.* New York: St. Martin's.

Craig, Clarence. 1953. *The First Epistle to the Corinthians. The Interpreter's Bible.* Vol. 10. Ed. G. A. Buttrick. New York: Abingdon.

Crook, J. A. 1967. *Law and Life in Rome, 90 B.C.–A.D. 212.* Ithaca: Cornell Univ.

Crouzel, Henri. 1978. "L'imitation et la 'suite' de Dieu et de Christ dans les premiers siècles chrétiens, ainsi que leurs sources gréco-romains et hébraiques." *JAC* 21:7-41.

Culler, Jonathan. 1982. *On Deconstruction: Theory and Criticism after Structuralism.* Ithaca: Cornell Univ.

D'Alton, J. F. 1931. *Roman Literary Theory and Criticism: A Study in Tendencies.* London: Longmans, Green.

Daly, Mary. 1973. *Beyond God the Father: Toward a Philosophy of Women's Liberation.* Boston: Beacon.

Delatte, L. 1942. *Les traités de la royauté d'Ecphante, Diotogène, et Sthénidas.* Bibliothèque de la Faculté de Philosophie et Lettres de l'Université de Liège 97. Liège: Droz.

Deleuze, Gilles. 1988. *Foucault.* Ed. and trans. Sean Hand. Minneapolis: Univ. of Minnesota.

Derrida, Jacques. 1976. *Of Grammatology.* Trans. Gayatri Chakravorty Spivak. Baltimore: Johns Hopkins Univ. French original: *De la grammatologie.* Paris: Minuit, 1967.

Diamond, Irene, and Lee Quinby, eds. 1988. *Feminism and Foucault: Reflections on Resistance*. Boston: Northeastern Univ.

Dibelius, Martin. 1937. *An die Thessalonicher I, II; An die Philipper*. 3d rev. ed. HNT. Ed. Hans Lietzmann. Tübingen: Mohr (Siebeck).

—— 1957-65. "Jesusbild der Gegenwart." *Religion in Geschichte und Gegenwart*³ 3:655-663.

—— 1971. *From Tradition to Gospel*. 2d rev. ed. Trans. Bertram Lee Wolff. Greenwood, SC: Attic.

Dick, K. 1900. *Der schriftstellerische Plural bei Paulus*. Halle: Niemeyer.

Dölger, Franz J., Hans Lietzmann, et al., eds. 1950ff. *Reallexicon für Antike und Christentum: Sachwörterbuch zur Auseinandersetzung des Christentum mit der antiken Welt*. Stuttgart: K. W. Hiersemann.

Döring, Klaus. 1979. *Exemplum Socratis: Studien zur Socratesnachwirkung in der kynisch-stoischen Popularphilosophie der frühen Kaiserzeit und im frühen Christentum*. Hermes: Zeitschrift für klassische Philologie 42. Wiesbaden: Steiner.

Dobschütz, E. von. 1909. *Die Thessalonicher-Briefe*. 7th ed. KEK. Göttingen: Vandenhoeck & Ruprecht.

Dreyfus, Hubert L. and Paul Rabinow. 1982. *Michel Foucault: Beyond Structuralism and Hermeneutics*. Chicago: Univ. of Chicago.

Dvornik, Francis. 1966. *Early Christian and Byzantine Political Philosophy: Origins and Background*. Dumbarton Oaks Studies 9. Washington: Dumbarton Oaks Center for Byzantine Studies.

Easterling, P. E. and B. M. W. Knox, eds. 1985. *The Cambridge History of Classical Literature*. Vol. 1: Greek Literature. Cambridge: Cambridge Univ.

Else, Gerald. 1958. "'Imitation' in the Fifth Century." *CP* 53:73-90.

Fantham, Elaine. 1978a. "Imitation and Decline: Rhetorical Theory and Practice in the First Century after Christ." *CP* 73:102-116.

—— 1978b. "Imitation and Evolution: The Discussion of Rhetorical Imitation in Cicero *De oratore* 2.87-97 and Some Related Problems of Ciceronian Theory." *CP* 73:1-16.

Fiore, Benjamin. 1982. *The Function of Personal Example in the Socratic and Pastoral Epistles*. Ph.D. Diss., Yale Univ.

Foucault, Michel. 1961. *Folie et déraison: histoire de la folie à l'âge classique*. Paris: Plon. Rev. ed.: *Histoire de la folie à l'âge classique*. Paris: Gallimard, 1972. ET of abridged ed.: *Madness and Civilization: A History of Insanity in the Age of Reason*. New York: Random House, 1965.

—— 1966. *Les mots et les choses: une archéologie des sciences humaines*. Paris: Gallimard. ET: *The Order of Things: An Archaeology of the Human Sciences*. New York: Pantheon, 1971.

Foucault, Michel (cont.). 1969. *L'archéologie du savoir*. Paris: Gallimard. ET: *The Archaeology of Knowledge*. Trans. A. M. Sheridan Smith. New York: Harper Colophon, 1976.

—— 1972. *Naissance de la clinique: Une archéologie du regard médical*. Rev. 2d ed. Paris: Presses Universitaires de France. ET: *The Birth of the Clinic: An Archaeology of Medical Perception*. Trans. Alan Sheridan Smith. New York: Pantheon, 1973.

—— 1975. *Surveiller et punir: Naissance de la prison*. Paris: Gallimard. ET: *Discipline and Punish: The Birth of the Prison*. Trans. Alan Sheridan. New York: Pantheon, 1977.

—— 1976. *Histoire de la sexualité*. Vol. 1: *La volonté de savoir*. Paris: Gallimard. ET: *The History of Sexuality*. Vol. 1: *Introduction*. Trans. Robert Hurley. New York: Vintage, 1980.

—— 1977. *Language, Counter-Memory, Practice: Selected Essays and Interviews*. Ed. Donald Bouchard. Trans. Donald Bouchard and Sherry Simon. Ithaca: Cornell Univ.

—— 1979. *Discipline and Punish: The Birth of the Prison*. Trans. Alan Sheridan. New York: Vintage.

—— 1980a. *Power/Knowledge: Selected Interviews and other Writings, 1972-1977*. Ed. Colin Gordon. Trans. Colin Gordon, et al. New York: Pantheon.

—— 1980b. "Body/Power." In Foucault 1980a:55-62.

—— 1980c. "The Confession of the Flesh." In Foucault 1980a:194-228.

—— 1980d. "Truth and Power." In Foucault 1980a:109-133.

—— 1980e. "Two Lectures." In Foucault 1980a:78-108.

—— 1982. "The Subject and Power." Afterword to Dreyfus and Rabinow 1982:208-226.

—— 1984a. *Histoire de la sexualité*. Vol. 2: *L'usage des plaisirs*. Paris: Gallimard. ET: *The Use of Pleasure*. Trans. Robert Hurley. New York: Pantheon, 1985.

—— 1984b. *Histoire de la sexualité*. Vol. 3: *Le souci de soi*. Paris: Gallimard. ET: *The Care of the Self*. Trans. Robert Hurley. New York: Pantheon, 1986.

—— 1988. *Politics, Philosophy, Culture: Interviews and Other Writings, 1977-1984*. Ed. Lawrence D. Kritzman. Trans. Alan Sheridan, et al. New York: Routledge.

Fraser, Nancy. 1989. *Unruly Practices: Power, Discourse and Gender in Contemporary Social Theory*. Minneapolis: Univ. of Minnesota.

Frischer, Bernard David. 1975. *At Tu Aureus Esto: Eine Interpretation von Vergils 7.Ekloge*. Bonn: Habelt.

—— 1982. *The Sculpted Word: Epicureanism and Philosophical Recruitment in Ancient Greece*. Berkeley: Univ. of California.

Frisk, Hjalmar. 1970. *Griechisches Etymologisches Wörterbuch*. Heidelberg: Winter.

Funk, Aloys. 1981. *Status und Rollen in den Paulusbriefen: Eine inhaltsanalytische Untersuchung zur Religionssoziologie*. Innsbrucker theologische Studien 7. Innsbruck: Tyrolia.

Furnish, Victor Paul. 1968. *Theology and Ethics in Paul*. Nashville: Abingdon.

—— 1985. *The Moral Teaching of Paul: Selected Issues*. Rev. ed. Nashville: Abingdon.

Gerhardsson, Birger. 1961. *Memory and Manuscript: Oral Tradition and Written Transmission in Rabbinic Judaism and Early Christianity*. Trans. Eric J. Sharpe. ASNU 22. Uppsala: Almquist & Wiksells.

Girard, René. 1978. *"To Double Business Bound": Essays on Literature, Mimesis, and Anthropology*. Baltimore: Johns Hopkins Univ.

Goodenough, Erwin R. 1928. "The Political Philosophy of Hellenistic Kingship." *Yale Classical Studies* 1:55-102.

Greene, W. C. 1918. "Plato's View of Poetry." *Harvard Studies in Classical Philology* 29:1-75.

Grundmann, W. 1971. "σύν." *TDNT* 7:766-798.

Guénel, Victor, ed. 1983. *Le corps et le corps du Christ dans la première épître aux Corinthiens*. Congrès de l'association catholique française pour l'étude de la Bible, Tarbes (1981). Lectio Divina 114. Paris: Cerf.

Gulin, E. G. 1925. "Die Nachfolge Gottes." *Studia Orientalia* 1:34-50.

Gutierrez, Pedro. 1968. *La paternité spirituelle selon Saint Paul*. Paris: Gabalda.

Hahm, David E. 1977. *The Origins of Stoic Cosmology*. Columbus: Ohio State Univ.

Hainz, Josef. 1972. *Ekklesia: Strukturen paulinischer Gemeinde Theologie und Gemeinde-Ordnung*. Biblische Untersuchungen 9. Regensburg: Pustet.

Haraway, Donna. 1988. "Reading Buchi Emecheta: Contests for Women's Experience in Women's Studies." *Inscriptions* 3/4: *Feminism and the Critique of Colonial Discourse*, 107-124.

Harootunian, H. D. 1988. "Foucault, Genealogy, History: The Pursuit of Otherness." In Arac 1988:110-137.

Hastings, James, ed. 1928. *Encyclopedia of Religion and Ethics*. New York: Charles Scribner's Sons.

Havelock, Eric. 1963. *Preface to Plato*. Cambridge: Harvard Univ.

Heitmann, A. 1940. *Imitatio Dei. Die ethische Nachahmung nach der Vaterlehre der zwei ersten Jahrhunderte*. Studia Anselmiana 10. Rome: Pontificium Institutum Anselmi.

Holmberg, Bengt. 1980. *Paul and Power: The Structure of Authority in the Primitive Church as Reflected in the Pauline Epistles*. Philadelphia: Fortress.

Hooker, Morna D. 1963-64. "'Beyond the Things Which Are Written':
    An Examination of I Cor. IV.6." *NTS* 10:127-132.
Hoy, David Couzens. 1986. *Foucault: A Critical Reader.* New York:
    Blackwell.
Hurd, John C. 1986. "The Authenticity of 1 Thess 2:13-16." Summary
    in *Abstracts: American Academy of Religion/Society of Biblical
    Literature 1986.* Decatur: Scholars.
Inscriptions. 1988. 3/4: *Feminism and the Critique of Colonial Dis-
    course.* Group for the Critical Study of Colonial Discourse.
    Santa Cruz: Univ. of California at Santa Cruz.
Jaeger, Werner. 1945. *Paideia: The Ideals of Greek Culture.* 3 vols. 2d.
    ed. Trans. Gilbert Highet. New York: Oxford Univ.
Kennedy, George. 1963. *The Art of Persuasion in Greece.* Princeton:
    Princeton Univ.
—— 1972. *The Art of Rhetoric in the Roman World, 300 B.C. - A.D.
    300.* Princeton: Princeton Univ.
—— 1980. *Classical Rhetoric and its Christian and Secular Tradition
    from Ancient to Modern Times.* Chapel Hill: Univ. of North
    Carolina.
King, Martin Luther, Jr. 1964. *Why We Can't Wait.* New York: Mentor.
Kirk, G.S., J. E. Raven, and M. Schofield. 1983. *The Presocratic
    Philosophers.* 2d ed. New York: Cambridge Univ.
Kittel, Gerhard. 1964. "ἀκολουθέω." *TDNT* 1:210-216.
—— 1964-74. (ed.) *Theological Dictionary of the New Testament.* 10
    vols. Trans. and ed. G. N. Bromiley. Grand Rapids: Eerdmanns.
Klaiber, Walter. 1982. *Rechtfertigung und Gemeinde: Eine Unter-
    suchung zum paulinischen Kirchenverstandnis.* FRLANT 127.
    Göttingen: Vandenhoeck & Ruprecht.
Koch, K. 1964. "L'imitation de Dieu dans la morale de l'Ancien
    Testament." *Studia Moralia* (Rome) 2:73-88.
Koller, Hans. 1954. *Die Mimesis in der Antike. Nachahmung, Darstel-
    lung, Ausdruck.* Dissertationes Bernenses, ser. 1, fasc. 5. Bern.
Koolmeister, Richard and Theodor Tallmeisther, comps. 1981. *An
    Index to Dio Chrysostomus.* Ed. Jan Fredrik Kindstrand. Stock-
    holm: Almquist & Wiksell.
LaDrière, Craig. 1939. "Horace and the Theory of Imitation." *Ameri-
    can Journal of Philology* 60:288-300.
Lagrange, Marie-Joseph. 1925. *Saint Paul, Epître aux Galates.* 2d ed.
    Etudes Bibliques. Paris: Gabalda.
Larsson, Edvin. 1962. *Christus als Vorbild: Eine Untersuchung zu den
    Paulinischen Tauf- und Eikontexten.* Uppsala: Almquist &
    Wiksells.
Lee, E. Kenneth. 1961-62. "Words Denoting 'Pattern' in the New
    Testament." *NTS* 8:166-173.

Liddell, Henry G. and Robert Scott. 1925-40. *A Greek-English Lexicon*. Rev. Henry S. Jones and Roderick McKenzie. 9th ed. Oxford: Clarendon.

Lietzmann, Hans. 1923. *An die Korinther I II*. 2d rev. ed. HNT 9. Tübingen: Mohr (Siebeck).

Lofthouse, W. F. 1953-54. "Imitatio Christi." *Exp Tim* 65:338-342.

Lohse, Eduard. 1957-65. "Nachfolge Christi." *Religion in Geschichte und Gegenwart*³ 4:1286-1288.

Long, A. A. 1974. *Hellenistic Philosophy*. New York: Charles Scribner's Sons.

Lyons, John D. and Stephen G. Nichols, Jr., eds. 1982. *Mimesis: From Mirror to Method, Augustine to Descartes*. Hanover: Univ. Press of New England.

Mack, Burton L. 1972. "*Imitatio Mosis*: Patterns of Cosmology and Soteriology in the Hellenistic Synagogue." *Studia Philonica* 1:27-55.

—— 1987. *A Myth of Innocence: Mark and Christian Origins*. Philadelphia: Fortress.

MacKendrick, Paul. 1960. *The Mute Stones Speak*. New York: Norton.

Mann, Michael. 1986. *The Sources of Social Power*. Vol. 1: *A History of Power from the Beginning to A.D. 1760*. New York: Cambridge Univ.

Marmorstein, A. 1928. "Die Nachahmung Gottes (*Imitatio Dei*) in der Agada." In *Judische Studien*, Festschrift J. Wehlgemuth. Pp. 1-16. Frankfurt im Maine: Kauffmann. ET: "The Imitation of God (*Imitatio Dei*) in the Haggadah." In *Studies in Jewish Theology, The Marmorstein Memorial Volume*. Ed. J. Rabbinowitz and M. S. Lew. Pp. 106-121. Oxford: Oxford Univ., 1950.

Marrou, Henri. 1982. *A History of Education in Antiquity*. Trans. George Lamb. Madison: Univ. of Wisconsin.

Martin, Biddy. 1988. "Feminism, Criticism, and Foucault." In Diamond and Quinby 1988:3-19.

Martin, Rux. 1988. "Truth, Power, Self: An Interview with Michel Foucault." In *Technologies of the Self: A Seminar with Michel Foucault*. Ed. Luther H. Martin, Huck Gutman, Patrick H. Hutton. Amherst: Univ. of Massachusetts.

Masson, Charles. 1957. *Les deux épîtres de Saint Paul aux Thessaloniciens*. CHT 11A. Neuchâtel: Delachaux et Niestlé.

Mayer, Günter. 1974. *Index Philoneus*. Berlin: de Gruyter.

McGrath, B. 1952. "'Syn'-Words in Paul." *CBQ* 14:219-226.

McKeon, Richard. 1936. "Literary Criticism and the Concept of Imitation in Antiquity." *Modern Philology* 34:1-35.

Meeks, Wayne A. 1983. *The First Urban Christians: The Social World of the Apostle Paul*. New Haven: Yale Univ.

Megill, Allan. 1985. *Prophets of Extremity: Nietzsche, Heidegger, Foucault, Derrida*. Berkeley: Univ. of California.

Merk, Otto. 1968. *Handeln aus Glauben: Die Motivierungen der paulinischen Ethik*. Marburg: Elwert.

Merki, H. 1952. *OMOIΩΣΙΣ ΘΕΩ. Von der Platonischen Angleichung an Gott zur Gottahnlichkeit bei Gregor von Nyssa*. Paradosis: Beitrage zur Geschichte der altchristlichen Literatur und Theologie 7. Freibourg: Paulusverlag.

Michaelis, W. 1967. "*μιμέομαι*." *TDNT* 4:659-674.

Moffatt, James. 1938. *The First Epistle of Paul to the Corinthians*. MNTC. New York: Harper.

Moore, Stephen D. 1989. *Literary Criticism and the Gospels: The Theoretical Challenge*. New Haven: Yale Univ.

Morris, Leon. 1959. *The First and Second Epistles to the Thessalonians*. NICNT. Grand Rapids: Eerdmanns.

Morrison, Karl F. 1982. *The Mimetic Tradition of Reform in the West*. Princeton: Princeton Univ.

Mudimbe, V. Y. 1988. *The Invention of Africa: Gnosis, Philosophy, and the Order of Knowledge*. Bloomington: Indiana Univ.

Munro, Winsome. 1983. *Authority in Paul and Peter: The Identification of a Pastoral Stratum in the Pauline Corpus and 1 Peter*. SNTSMS 45. New York: Cambridge Univ.

Neil, William. 1950. *The Epistle of Paul to the Thessalonians*. MNTC. New York: Harper.

Nicholas, Barry. 1962. *An Introduction to Roman Law*. Oxford: Clarendon.

Nielen, J. M. 1938. "Die Kultsprache der Nachfolge und Nachahmung Gottes und verwandter Bezeichnungen in neutestamentlichen Schrifttum." In *Heilige Überlieferung: Ausschnitte aus der Geschichte des Mönchtums und des heiligen Kultes* (Festschrift Ildefons Herwegen). Pp. 59-85. Münster: Aschendorff.

North, Helen. 1966. *Sophrosyne: Self-Knowledge and Self-Restraint in Greek Literature*. Cornell Studies in Classical Philology 35. Ithaca: Cornell Univ.

Ochshorn, Judith. 1981. *The Female Experience and the Nature of the Divine*. Bloomington: Indiana Univ.

Oepke, Albrecht. 1937. *Der Brief des Paulus an die Galater*. Ed. Joachim Rohde. THKNT 9. Berlin: Evangelische Verlagsanstalt.

Organ, Troy Wilson. 1949. *An Index to Aristotle*. Princeton: Princeton Univ.

Parry, R. 1916. *The First Epistle of Paul the Apostle to the Corinthians*. Cambridge: Cambridge Univ.

Patte, Daniel. 1983. *Paul's Faith and the Power of the Gospel: A Structural Introduction to the Pauline Letters*. Philadelphia: Fortress.

Pearson, Birger. 1971. "I Thessalonians 2:13-16: A Deutero-Pauline Interpolation." *HTR* 64:79-94.

Petersen, Norman R. 1985. *Rediscovering Paul: Philemon and the Sociology of Paul's Narrative World*. Philadelphia: Fortress.

Pohlenz, M. 1955-58. *Die Stoa: Geschichte einer geistigen Bewegung*. 2 vols. Göttingen: Vandenhoeck & Ruprecht.

Prellwitz, Walter. 1905. *Etymologisches Wörterbuch der griechischen Sprache*. 2d ed. Göttingen: Vandenhoeck & Ruprecht.

Price, Bennett J. 1975. ΠΑΡΑΔΕΙΓΜΑ *and* EXEMPLUM *in Ancient Rhetorical Theory*. Ph.D. Diss., Univ. of California at Berkeley.

Proudfoot, C. M. 1963. "Imitation or Realistic Participation? A Study of Paul's Concept of 'Suffering with Christ'." *Int* 17:140-160.

Reale, Giovanni. 1985. *The Systems of the Hellenistic Age: A History of Ancient Philosophy*. Trans. and ed. John R. Catan. Albany: State Univ. of New York.

Reich, Hermann. 1903. *Der Mimus: Ein litterar-entwickelungsgeschichtlicher Versuch*. Berlin: Weidmann.

Rengstorf, Karl Heinrich, ed. 1979. *A Complete Concordance to Flavius Josephus*. Leiden: Brill.

Rigaux, Béda. 1950. *Saint Paul: Les Epîtres aux Thessaloniciens*. Paris: Gabalda.

Riley, Denise. 1988. *"Am I That Name?" Feminism and the Category of "Women" in History*. Minneapolis: Univ. of Minnesota.

Robertson, Archibald and Alfred Plummer. 1914. *The First Epistle of St. Paul to the Corinthians*. 2d ed. IDD. Edinburgh: Clark.

Roloff, Jürgen. 1965. *Apostolat-Verkündigung-Kirche: Ursprung, Inhalt und Funktion des kirchlichen Apostelamtes nach Paulus, Lukas und den Pastoralbriefen*. Gutersloh: Mohn.

Rosen, Stanley. 1983. *Plato's Sophist: The Drama of Original and Image*. New Haven: Yale Univ.

Russell, D. A. 1981. *Criticism in Antiquity*. Berkeley: Univ. of California.

Russell, D. A. and M. Winterbottom, eds. 1972. *Ancient Literary Criticism: The Principal Texts in New Translations*. Oxford: Clarendon.

Rutenber, Culbert Gerow. 1946. *The Doctrine of the Imitation of God in Plato*. Morningside Heights: King's Crown.

Sanders, Boykin. 1981. "Imitating Paul: 1 Cor 4:16." *HTR* 74:353-363.

Schlier, Heinrich. 1949. *Der Brief an die Galater*. 10th ed. KEK. Göttingen: Vandehoeck & Ruprecht.

Schmid, Wilhelm and Otto Stählin. 1929. *Geschichte der griechischen Literatur, I:1: Die griechische Literatur vor der attischen Hegemonie*. Handbuch der Altertumswissenschaft 7. München: Beck.

Schmid, Wolfgang. 1951. "Götter und Menschen in der Theologie Epikurs." *Rheinisches Museum für Philologie* 94:97-156.

Schmithals, Walter. 1969. *The Office of Apostle in the Early Church.* Trans. John E. Steely. Nashville: Abingdon.

Schnackenburg, Rudolf. 1965. *The Moral Teaching of the New Testament.* Trans. J. Holland-Smith and W. J. O'Hara. New York: Seabury.

Schneider, Johannes. 1971. "μετασχηματίζω." *TDNT* 7:957-958.

Schoeps, H. J. 1950. *Aus Frühchristlicher Zeit. Religionsgeschichtliche Untersuchungen.* Tübingen: Mohr (Siebeck).

Schüssler Fiorenza, Elisabeth. 1984. *In Memory of Her: A Feminist Theological Reconstruction of Christian Origins.* New York: Crossroads.

Schütz, John Howard. 1975. *Paul and the Anatomy of Apostolic Authority.* SNTSMS 26. New York: Cambridge Univ.

Schulz, Anselm. 1962. *Nachfolgen und Nachahmung: Studien über das Verhaltnis der neutestamentlichen Jungerschaft zur Urchristlichen Vorbildethik.* SANT 6. München: Kosel.

Schulze, Wilhelm. 1966. *Kleine Schriften.* 2d aug. ed. Göttingen: Vandenhoeck & Ruprecht.

Schwyzer, Eduard. 1939. *Griechische Grammatik.* Handbuch der Altertumwissenschaft II:1. München: Beck.

Scott, Joan Wallach. 1988. "The Sears Case." In *Gender and the Politics of History.* Pp. 167-177. New York: Columbia Univ.

Shaw, Graham. 1983. *The Cost of Authority: Manipulation and Freedom in the New Testament.* Philadelphia: Fortress.

Sontag, Susan. 1966. *"Against Interpretation" and Other Essays.* New York: Farrar Straus Giroux.

Sörbom, Göran. 1966. *Mimesis and Art: Studies in the Origin and Early Development of an Aesthetic Vocabulary.* Uppsala: Appelbergs.

Spariosu, Mihai. 1984a. *Literature, Mimesis and Play: Essays in Literary Theory.* Philadelphia: John Benjamins.

—— 1984b. *Mimesis in Contemporary Theory: An Interdisciplinary Approach. I: The Literary and Philosophical Debate.* Cultura Ludens: Imitation and Play in Western Culture I:1. Philadelphia: John Benjamins.

Stanley, D. M. 1959. "Become imitators of me. The Pauline Conception of Apostolic Tradition." *Bib* 40:859-877.

Stowers, Stanley Kent. 1981. *The Diatribe and Paul's Letter to the Romans.* SBLDS 57. Chico: Scholars.

Sturz, Friedrich G. 1964. *Lexicon Xenophonteum.* Repr. ed. 4 vols. Hildesheim: Olms.

Tarde, G. 1895. *Les lois de l'imitation: Etude Sociologique.* 2d. rev. & aug. ed. Paris: Felix Alcan.

Tate, J. 1928. "'Imitation' in Plato's *Republic.*" *CQ* 22:16-23.

—— 1932. "Plato and Imitation." *CQ* 26:161-169.

Thysman, R. 1966. "L'ethique de l'imitation du Christ dans le Nouveau Testament. Stutation, notations et variations du theme." *ETL* 42:138-175.

Tinsley, E. H. 1960. *The Imitation of God in Christ. An Essay on the Biblical Basis of Christian Spirituality.* London: SCM.

Trible, Phyllis. 1978. *God and the Rhetoric of Sexuality.* Philadelphia: Fortress.

Trinh T. Minh-Ha. 1988. "Not You/Like You: Post-Colonial Women and the Interlocking Questions of Identity and Difference." *Inscriptions 3/4: Feminism and the Critique of Colonial Discourse,* 71-77. Reprinted in *Making Face, Making Soul=Haciendo Caras: Creative and Critical Perspectives by Women of Color.* Pp. 371-375. Ed. Gloria Anzaldúa. San Francisco: Aunt Lute Foundation Books, 1990.

―――― 1989. *Woman, Native, Other: Writing Postcoloniality and Feminism.* Bloomington: Indiana Univ.

Verdenius, Willem J. 1949. *Mimesis: Plato's Doctrine of Artistic Imitation and its Meaning for Us.* Philosophia Antiqua 3. Leiden: Brill.

Vogel, C. J. de. 1966. *Pythagoras and Early Pythagoreanism: An Interpretation of Neglected Evidence on the Philosopher Pythagoras.* Assen: Van Gorcum.

Wallis, P. 1950. "Ein neuer Auslegungsversuch der Stelle I. Kor 4,6." *TLZ* 75:506-508.

Webster. 1988. *Webster's Ninth New Collegiate Dictionary.* Springfield, MA: Merriam-Webster.

Weiss, Johannes. 1925. *Der erste Korintherbrief.* 10th ed. KEK. Göttingen: Vandenhoeck & Ruprecht.

Wendland, H.-D. 1980. *Die Briefe an die Korinther.* 15 Aufl. Das Neue Testament Deutsch 7. Göttingen: Vandenhoeck & Ruprecht.

White, Hayden. 1978. "Foucault Decoded: Notes from Underground." In *Tropics of Discourse: Essays in Cultural Criticism.* Pp. 230-260. Baltimore: Johns Hopkins Univ.

Williams, Donald Manly. 1967. *The Imitation of Christ in Paul with Special Reference to Paul as Teacher.* Ph.D. Diss., Columbia Univ.

Williams, Gordon. 1978. *Change and Decline: Roman Literature in the Early Empire.* Berkeley: Univ. of California.

Wolin, Sheldon S. 1988. "On the Theory and Practice of Power." In Arac 1988:179-201.

INDEXES

MODERN AUTHORS

BIBLICAL AND INTERTESTAMENTAL LITERATURE

ANCIENT SOURCES

Made in the USA
Lexington, KY
30 August 2016